WHAT PEOPLE ARE SAYING ABOUT
The Soul Factor
by Shelley Maurice-Maier

"As a family practice and emergency physician for more than 25 years, I have always struggled with connecting the soul and spirit of the person with their physical symptoms and illnesses. Our modern American medical training has almost completely isolated the physical from the soul/spirit, and tends to turn medical professionals into testing and prescribing technologists. Better living through chemistry and cutting dominates the medical scene today. Shelley's book is unique in that the true connection of body-soul-Spirit with respect to suffering and disease is practically spelled out in multitudes of anecdotes from her own life and that of her clients. I pray I may learn from her experience and hard work of pointing the soul to Christ."

ALBERT D. BRAUER, M.D.
PASCO, WASHINGTON

"After twenty years of working with people who are hurting, *The Soul Factor* is the book I've been looking for. Drawing heavily from her own life and her work as a counselor, Maurice-Maier skillfully ties together the strings of science and salvation to show the clear role of the soul in finding freedom and hope that lasts. This is the rare "quick read" that actually plows new ground and delivers not just good ideas, but real action steps for real change."

BO STERN
PASTOR, BEND, OREGON

As I read *The Soul Factor,* I can hear Shelley's words of health and wholeness from when we led our workshops on *The Sampler* together. She honestly shares her painful, but victorious story (which bypasses our defenses) about truths of how our thinking greatly influences our choices, behavior, emotions, physical health and our spiritual health.

As a therapist, she works with the whole person. From her experience with the mind/body/Spirit connection, she gives us practical ways of learning to choose health for our Soul as we let God be at the helm of our Sanctification Voyage. I can't wait to read it again for my own sanctification process, and share *The Soul Factor* with my clients."

BARBARA M. HOUSTON, PSYD.
LICENSED PSYCHOLOGIST, CANBY, OR

"When confronted by Jesus, the Author of wholeness, the demons who possessed a shattered soul from Gadarenes confessed through their tenant's mouth, 'My name is Legion.' A Roman legion was made up of five thousand soldiers. This poor man was broken in five thousand pieces. (See Mark 5:1-20) That's a sad picture of human disintegration. How we need the progressive wholeness and wellness that Jesus Christ brought to this man and can bring to us!

"Shelley Maurice-Maier shares with transparent honesty, the importance of each person's journey toward becoming more and more like Jesus, the Author of wholeness. She shares through her personal journey as well as her experiences as a therapist, the mind/body/Spirit connection in our journey toward physical, psychological and spiritual wellness."

KEN JOHNSON
SENIOR PASTOR, WESTSIDE CHURCH
BEND, OREGON

"The Soul Factor" is an amazing little book that connects scientific truth with spiritual truth to provide powerful insights into how we can live our lives more effectively—how to experience both greater physical and spiritual health.

"Shelley accomplishes this by illustrating the truths she is sharing with candid, transparent, and sometimes painful experiences from her own life story. This is the only book I know of that reveals the link between the medical insights into the Mind-body Connection with the spiritual process of Sanctification. This is a 'must read' book!"

RETIRED PASTOR, DONALD G. STEWART, PHD
CHRISTIAN LIFE COACH, BEND, OREGON

"In her book, Shelley exudes her personal transparency and Biblical wisdom. *The Soul Factor* is a valuable reminder that as we allow God to guide us in the sanctification process we must wholeheartedly submit our body/mind/soul to Jesus."

BOB HAKALA, MD
PHYSICIAN OF THE YEAR
OREGON ACADEMY OF FAMILY PRACTICE

"What I especially like about Shelley is her honesty about her own struggles in life. *The Soul Factor* reads just like her counseling—tremendous insight into how God intended life to work—mined from the many shipwrecks she has personally experienced.

"Even though I have five years of post-graduate study at Multnomah & Western Seminary, I had never seen Shelley's insight in the process of Sanctification using the mind/body/Spirit, with the emphasis on the work of the Holy Spirit's role in our own Sanctification. Truth is best remembered in the context of stories, which Jesus demonstrated during His ministry here on Earth. *The Soul Factor* will entertain you with incredible stories and personable Biblical applications that will leap off the pages at you. You will 'get it.' If these principals can work for a flawed, fellow traveler like Shelley, they can surely work for the rest of us."

ROGER A. ELLIS
MASTER OF DIVINITY

"This book communicates masterfully the incredible and powerful connection between our mind, body, and Spirit and God's great purposes and plans for us. I promise that your life and walk with God will be beautifully and forever changed as you incorporate these amazing truths into your daily life."

CLAIRE ELLIS
RN, PHN, BSN

"The Soul Factor brings a positive, hopeful and practical message to the reader. I was especially reminded of the exquisite importance of positive, forgiving thoughts on our overall well-being. I think I need to be reminded that the idea of negative, punishing thoughts are not just annoying background noise. If left unchecked, they will affect the physical body to its detriment. Shelley's unflinching honesty will inspire people to take those voices seriously and address what needs to be done."

QUINN SCALLON, MD
MOSAIC MEDICAL
BEND, OREGON

"I finished reading *The Soul Factor* last night before going to bed. After sleeping for a couple of hours, I woke up thinking about the book and about what came through to me most clearly from your stories and from all the good information in the book.

"It came to me that I need to think in agreement with the things I know God has said to me, the things I know God has purposed for me, and the things that are good for me.

"So I spent about an hour forming thoughts about me, my wife, my ministry, my future, my health, God's provision. I formed those thoughts into positive statements and I thought about them clearly.

Thanks for the instruction and inspiration."

JIM STEVENS
MINISTRY PASTOR, WESTSIDE CHURCH
BEND, OREGON

"This is a great read for people who need help (like me) or people who have the privilege to speak into other people's lives. I found myself challenged one minute and in the next minute Shelley was putting to pen ideas and concepts I have wrestled with and was never able to verbalize."

GREG PRICE
PASTOR, CRESCENT CHURCH, OREGON

THE SOUL FACTOR

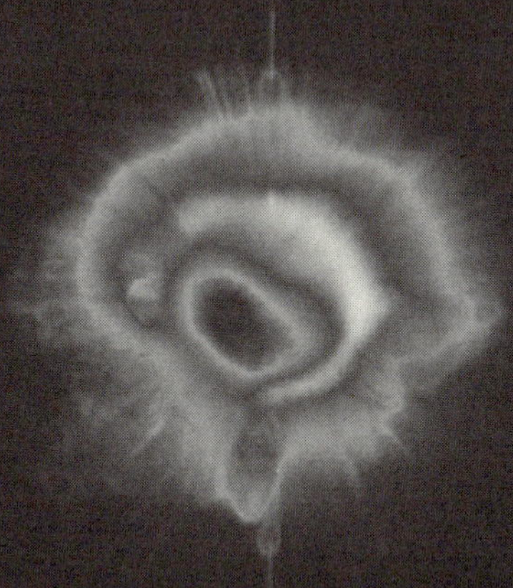

SHELLEY MAURICE - MAIER

ABIDING BOOKS

Abiding Books
www.abidingbooks.com
The Soul Factor
© 2009 by Shelley Maurice-Maier
All rights reserved. Published 2009
Printed in the United States of America

ALL RIGHTS RESERVED
No part of this publication may be reproduced, stored in a retrieval system, or transmitted, in any form or by any means—electronic, mechanical, photocopying, recording, or otherwise—without prior written permission.

ISBN: 978-0-9744284-7-5

A CIP catalog record for this book is available from the Library of Congress.

Cover and art design by Gavran Digital Art.
www.gavrandigitalart.com

Interior design and typeset by Pamela McGrew.

Dedication

To my beloved husband, Ken, whose continued, living example of 1 Corinthians 13:4–8 has helped heal and inspire me to seek God's truth and love in a deeper way.

Thank you for believing in and investing in God's message of hope and healing through me so that it might live on in this book.

To Debbie Newman, my friend since childhood and my sister in Christ, who first invited me to know the Lord personally—and what a difference it has made in our lives!

To Sue Kay, for the many hours of laughter and tears we shared while refining sentences and selecting the most appropriate and descriptive scriptures to include with them.

Thank you, also, for the example you have set for me in living out the precepts in this book.

To Dr. Don Stewart, retired Pastor, our dear friend and mentor.

Thank you for tireless hours of editorial support, which helped clarify and simplify the foundational theology behind the communication of my personal experience with Christ.

To Judith St. Pierre, Linden Gross, and Sue Spillane-Bramlette for the application of your literary skills, teaching, and encouragement to me to stick with the writing challenge. Without you, this book would not have advanced to publication.

And to those friends, Fred Austin, Jim Chauncey, Roger Ellis, Norma Mueller, Clyde Thompson, and publicist Sharon Cook, who read and offered honest criticism and suggestions, I thank you. Your points were thoughtful, excellent, and used to great advantage throughout the writing of *The Soul Factor*.

Contents

Foreword: A Voyage of Discovery 1

1. My Maiden Voyage
   The Need for Vigilance and a Compass 11

2. The Wrong Course
   Resetting My Compass...19

3. The Great Rescue
   A New Course..31

4. An Anchor for the Soul
   Behaviors Are Tied to Thoughts 41

5. Taking the Wind out of Fear's Sails
   With God, All Things Are Possible 51

6. Sunken Treasure
   Focusing on God Fills My Heart 65

7. Swimming against the Tide
   What You Expect, You Will Realize 77

8. Controlling the Rudder
   The Tongue Sets the Course of Your Life 89

9. Steering by a True Compass
   It May be Our Truth, But Is It the Truth? 101

10. Sailing Upright
    Proper Maintenance Makes for a Seaworthy Ship 107

11. Storms and Treacherous Shoals
    The Fullness of God's Love Is Revealed in Suffering 119

12. At the Helm
    Who's in Control? 131

    Epilogue: The Ultimate Quest
    Glorifying God Is the Soul's True Purpose 141

FOREWORD

A Voyage of Discovery

*"I pray that you may enjoy good health,
even as your soul is getting along well."*

—3 JOHN 1, NIV

Greek mythology tells of two deadly sea monsters that dwelt on opposite sides of a narrow strait. Scylla hid beneath a rock on one side. Charybdis lurked in a whirlpool on the other. Between them they posed a serious threat of survival to passing sea vessels. Ship captains knew if they sailed too close to Scylla, she would swoop down and devour them. If they sailed too close to Charybdis, she would suck them under the sea.

Similarly, obstacles to our faith in a loving God lie in wait to consume us and sometimes plunge us down into dangerous, life-threatening spiritual territory. For me, the phrase "between Scylla and Charybdis" has come to mean that navigating a life of faith is something like a ship's passage through treacherous narrows, gliding forward slowly while trying to avoid *Scylla* on the one side and *Charybdis* on the other. *How can we hope to accomplish this?*

Clearly, we cannot trust even our own limited vision of reality, so often clouded by a human perspective of the world, to keep us safe from predatory diversions. Only steering by the compass of God's truth—*real truth*—can guide us safely past Scylla and Charybdis. The unerring truths that keep us safe on this *voyage of discovery* are these: 1) God's Spirit works to bring health and wholeness to all aspects of our being, and, 2) He wants us to cooperate in the process by fixing our eyes on *His* compass point settings.

The Soul Factor discusses the importance of man's journey toward Sanctification (or, as *Webster's Dictionary* defines it, "freedom from error and the state of being set aside to a higher, sacred purpose") through both the mind/body/Spirit [notice, that is, "Holy Spirit"] principles that promote spiritual health *and* the part our own soul plays in moving us toward this corrective, healing state of being.

As we embark on a voyage toward greater understanding of the mind/body/Spirit connection and of Sanctification, I am well aware of the hidden dangers that lurk above and below these waters. After all, I spent much of my early life bouncing back and forth between Scylla and Charybdis: inner temptation and outward danger. As you seek to fulfill God's plan for your own life, I pray this little book may help enlighten and encourage you so you may not take as long as I did to get your life firmly on course.

God: My Personal Coast Guard Captain?

From a young age I believed in God and counted on Him to rescue me in the "rainstorms" of daily experience. Like a small ship bobbing over steep waves in open water, my ship was often in distress due to poor maintenance on my part or my neglect to follow the simple, fixed compass settings on His heavenly nautical chart that make for a safe journey. I behaved as if God were either my "Santa Claus in the Sky," bringing me gifts and surprises, or my "personal Coast Guard Captain"—there when I drifted into deep waters and called out to Him in desperation. I really didn't understand what it meant to be a Christian or to have a two-way relationship with my Creator.

At thirty I discovered God was more than my *personal life preserver*. A friend helped me see I needed not only to *acknowledge* but to make an interactive commitment to the Lord. I accepted then that what Jesus had done on the Cross—*defeat death*—was actually done for me, so that I could have eternal life. This was great for about six months. Yet even then I ignored the warning buoys telling me of my need to develop a deeper relationship with Jesus. What I had was an infatuation. I was in love with the idea that Jesus loved me, but was not taking action on truly loving *Him*.

Like the story in Mark, Chapter Four, which tells of the seed that is sown on ground that looks rich and fertile but lacks depth because of the rocks that lie just beneath the surface, my "grounding" was shallow. It contained thorns—worries, poor decisions, and lifestyle problems—so when the first young blades of grass... *growth*...in my spirit began to poke through, thorns choked out what little I *was* learning about Jesus. His life was there, but there was no way to yield a good crop when I was not firmly rooted. Time passed, and though I still *believed* in Jesus, after awhile I was no longer "in love with" or sailing closely beside Him.

A Spiritual Undertow

It took two decades for me to realize there was a *next step* of faith to be taken. I needed to know God was more than a super-powered Coast Guard speedboat Captain whose sole purpose was to respond to my ongoing and frequent "Maydays." Jesus was *God*. He had a personalized ship's manifest for me, one that would reveal His purpose for launching my voyage. God's first compass points, His first and second commandments, would be good starting points in getting my little boat on course. They instructed me to:

Love the Lord your God with all your heart, with all your soul, with all your strength, and with all your mind. And love your neighbor as yourself. (Luke 10:27)

Once I'd decided to believe in Jesus Christ as my personal Savior, I found I had help in becoming the person God intended me to be. The Holy Spirit, whom Jesus sent to all those who believed in Him following His Resurrection, took up residence within and subtly guided me. I began to live out the plan He unfolded daily as I spoke with God, studied His Word, and spent time with other seekers. I soon got on course with the Holy Spirit's trade winds and entered into the process of *Sanctification*.

Simply defined, *Sanctification* is the progressive journey of growing into someone more and more like Jesus. We do this by choosing to set ourselves apart from a secular worldview and seeking a spiritual one. In living "in the world, but not of the world," in behaving differently from the secular world's values and lifestyles, we change. We become a new person and find ourselves more frequently in the center of God's will. We look into the Face of God, reflect His glory, and begin to display His Holiness in our lives. To do so, we must understand the things that are God's will for each person. Scripture gives many references that make it very clear what God wills for us all. Here are just a few:

- Be saved: 1 Timothy 2:3, 4
- Be filled with the Spirit: Ephesians 5:18
- Be sanctified: 1 Thessalonians 4:3
- Be submitted to laws and rulers: 1 Peter 2:13–15
- Be willing to suffer: 1 Peter 2:20, 21; 3:17, and 5:10
- Be thankful: 1 Thessalonians 5:18

Even after I'd sincerely accepted Christ as a personal Friend and Companion in my life, I was not able to feel God's complete forgiveness. My lack of understanding of the process of Sanctification kept me from knowing more of what He had in mind. I continued to harbor the negative perceptions that resulted from painful past experiences: long-term and serious health issues, early childhood abuse, and poor choices in my life.

Once I embraced *my* role in the Sanctification process and understood that God provided the Holy Spirit—*Jesus in me*—to help, I began to understand what to do and how to do it. When I understood the role *our soul* must actively play in this lifelong process, I could get started. *But what is the soul,* I wondered.

I came to understand that our soul is defined as the sum total of our thoughts (intellect), emotions, and will. Our soul is the only aspect of our being over which we have true influence. It is one of God's gifts, one that everyone possesses. I learned that with the guidance and power of the Holy Spirit, speaking to my soul through my own spirit, I could incline my thoughts, emotions, and will toward Him through cooperation and actively *yield* to His Word. Otherwise, I would be inclining my thoughts, emotions, and will to the judgments and dictates of the secular world. The choice was mine. I called this active choice for (or against) Sanctification the "soul factor."

As I read His Word daily and asked for His guidance through prayer, God began to show me His greater plan and purpose for my life. I learned I could be healed, regardless of the state of my body. Eventually I would share with my counseling clients, friends, family members, and those I taught through workshops and retreats, that there was hope and healing for anyone who desired change in their physical, psychological, or spiritual state. Anyone who *chose* to be could be sanctified! Yet God helped me understand how we are invited to *cooperate with His Spirit* in this process. This "will" piece is often the missing one in the mind/body/Spirit connection. When we don't actively cooperate with and align our will with God's Spirit, we won't grow in sanctity, health, and healing. After all, God gave mankind free will. He waits for us to choose His will freely as a sign of our love and trust in Him.

Choosing God's will over our own takes a daily commitment to reset our natural, secular way of thinking to align with His *compass point* settings. These are God's preset *default settings* on our ship's computer, from which the pull of *secular world* values can cause us to depart. Once we are willing to replace the old thoughts, habits, and behaviors from a godless worldview, we want to add new habits, thoughts, and behaviors from the spiritual worldview. To keep our understanding of God's truths current and on course requires frequent course correction. By realigning ourselves with God's Spirit frequently, we can avoid returning to the old ways of thinking.

Are You Satisfied with Your Relationship to God?

As a maturing Christian and practicing counselor, I use the truths of Scripture and my understanding of the mind/body/Spirit connection—that each element impacts the others—to help people reach their goals and experience spiritual growth. Together, the mind, the body, and the Spirit of God are essential components when it comes to following through with the Holy Spirit's desire for us to participate in our own process. In doing so, we begin to live the abundant life Jesus promised us.

The mind/body/Spirit connection plays an integral part in our journey toward physical, psychological, and spiritual wellness. In 1975, the medical community coined the term *Psychoneuroimmunology* (PNI). Medical research provided scientific evidence that there is a connection between the psychological, neurological, and immunological functions of our bodies. This *magnificent connection* describes the correlation between *what we think* and our ability to help heal ourselves. To my knowledge, no one has explored the Christian perspective of Sanctification with respect to the role the Holy Spirit plays in the mind/body connection. I feel it's important to understand, and this is the subject of the book you're about to read.

There are two questions that helped me embark on my own journey toward Sanctification, questions you may want to ask yourself, as well. *Would you say you are satisfied with your relationship with God?* And, *do you think God is satisfied with your relationship with Him?*

No matter how you answer these questions, know that Sanctification is a process that takes us through both calm waters and across rough seas throughout our entire lives. Whether the way is calm or rough, the Lord Himself is with us on our journey, watching over us, interested in every challenge we face. When we take our first step of faith with a will to grow and heal, the Holy Spirit comes in to strengthen and guide us, unfailingly, toward our true purpose and destiny.

ONE

My Maiden Voyage
The Need for Vigilance and a Compass

"I can see that our voyage is going to be disastrous
And bring great loss to ship and cargo,
and to our own lives, also."

—ACTS 27:10, THE APOSTLE PAUL

I marveled at the grace and confidence of the seagulls hovering just above me, within arm's reach, just outside of the wheelhouse. The sunlight and sea air were so captivating! When the flock landed on deck, pecking morsels of bait out of Mark's hand, I was thrilled to the core of my being. Surveying the blue expanse of water out beyond our vessel, I did some deep knee bends, then leaned down to rummage through my sea bag for an emery board, intent on sinking into the captain's chair to file my nails. I was having so much fun, in fact, that my mind wandered off course—and my *body* soon followed.

Suddenly our boat pitched. I lost balance and fell to the floor. Before I could get back on my feet, the boat lurched forward again. Mark rushed in behind me, shouting.

"Reverse throttle! Reverse the engine!"

Stunned, I sat frozen where I'd fallen. Mark catapulted over me and thrust back the throttle. Too late! We'd run aground on a shoal more than a mile out from shore. I resorted to a "Mayday" prayer: *"Father in heaven, please help us!"*

"What's the tide doing?" Mark asked in a strained voice.

"The tide?" I asked. "What do you mean, 'the tide?'"

"Where's the tide book?" he continued, earnestly." I need to know if the tide is coming in or going out."

My stomach sank. Mark had asked me to study the tide book, but the water had been so rough I'd just thrown it in a drawer and forgotten about it. Now I fumbled around in the drawer, in desperate search of it, and placed it in Mark's hands.

"Why is it so important to know what the tide is doing right now?" I asked. "It's early morning—and the sun won't set until after ten o'clock tonight. We have enough food to last awhile, and *someone* will come along and help us, right?"

"Look," Mark answered curtly, searching through the book. "There's at least a twenty-foot tidal variance every twelve hours this time of year. This is a wooden boat. She has run aground, and that will most likely split open some of her major seams. Our bilge pump isn't big enough to handle taking on much water. We have no skiff or dry suits. We have a nine-foot displacement hull, which means that if the tide is going out, we will eventually keel over. Then, when the tide comes in, we'll rapidly fill up with water. I don't know how much time we have, so if the tide *is* going out I'll need to cut down the mast and use it to shore up the hull. I don't even know if I brought an ax. *Now do you understand?"*

Mortified and becoming really frightened, I said, "Maybe we should call the Coast Guard to come help us."

"No! I won't call out a Mayday. I've skippered large ships for a living. I'd rather drown than be disgraced over grounding this little thirty-six-foot boat."

I silently prayed more *prayers of desperation*. Mark found the page containing the information he needed. The tide, it seemed, was coming *in* now. Relieved, Mark headed into the hold to review the damages. Returning a few minutes later, he reported that several seams in her hull had opened and that our small bilge pump was already overwhelmed. We'd have to start hauling up water from the hold in order to keep it from flooding the engine—and our boat from sinking!

We bailed from below decks for more than an hour. Fortunately, we kept the water level in the hold below our shins until the rising tide could finally set us afloat. One of us bailed and the other stood at the wheel as we slowly made our way back to dry dock at Wrangle, where at last we could caulk the split seams and repair the broken propeller.

More Than a Lesson on Fishing

Just two days before our near-disaster I still felt eager to do things women at thirty-four years of age weren't usually expected to do. On this five-day voyage up Alaska's inside passage my husband of three years was going to teach me how to *pot fish* for spotted shrimp and how to navigate a boat. When we left Ketchikan he'd promised to teach me the ropes as we went along and asked me to familiarize myself with the tide book, navigational charts, and the workings of the radio, compass, and depth-finder.

On the second day of our voyage a storm hit. I hadn't had time to acquire sea legs yet, and the rolling and pitching made me deathly nauseous. Besides, I had no desire to read about the things Mark had told me to study. I felt too sick and too scared. I prayed to God He would get us safely across Queen Charlotte Sound, and He did.

I got a good night's sleep and awoke the next morning feeling much better. After breakfast Mark told me to stand watch and steer the F/V *Silkie* at an idle toward a small island about three miles ahead off her bow. He warned me there were shoals well out from shore, which could make for a treacherous passage. Although the island was an excellent visual landmark, I would have to depend on the *exact* compass heading in order to stay on course. Even the slightest variation could cause us to go aground.

"No problem," I'd said. Mark confidently left me at the wheel while he stepped onto the back deck to chop up frozen crabmeat for the bait jars.

About thirty minutes later, when the diesel engine had warmed up sufficiently, Mark poked his head into the wheelhouse and told me to push the throttle forward until we were making about six knots per hour. With little effort on my part, the throttle glided forward. The engine immediately responded and the sea began to slap noisily against the hull as we moved on a straight course to the island, until my irreverence for keeping vigil over the correct compass setting caused our vessel to go aground. *Do Scylla and Charybdis sound familiar?*

I see my maiden voyage on the *F/V Silkie* as a metaphor for most of my Christian experience. For many years after I accepted God's offer of Salvation through His Son, Jesus Christ, I continually veered off course, then prayed that God would rescue me.

I knew that I was on a spiritual journey as a Christian. And, as I traveled along, I eventually learned life-enhancing principles that helped keep me on course and get me past the "shoals" along the way. Applying those principles to my life taught me more about God and helped me experience hope and healing on my journey. They gave me the spiritual concepts and content that led to my first book, *The Sampler*.

I came to see God was trying to teach me even more. While I sought to plot a course through life by focusing on my personal goals, God wanted me to start navigating by the *new compass* He'd given me as a gift at my new birth. Only by submitting my soul more fully to God could I follow the course that would ultimately transform me into the image of Jesus Himself. Although I was a sincere and believing Christian, I had yet to understand that until I intentionally, vigilantly, and continually surrendered my soul to God, I would never realize His greater purpose for my life. These days, I no longer consider myself to be on a journey. Now I know I'm on a *quest. What is the difference?*

On a journey we can choose just to sit back and enjoy the scenery until we reach our destination, much as I was trying to do on my *maiden voyage*. On a journey, we can rest on our oars and drift a bit, or even file our nails. Though we risk running aground now and then with such a careless approach to our destination, we hope that God will rescue us. I'm sure I drifted forward in my spiritual life in this manner for too many years.

I now think God wants more *for* us and *from* us. I

believe He intends for us to live the Christian life with every part of our being *fully engaged* in pursuing Him and His will for us. When our journey becomes a quest, we want to expend a constant, conscious, concentrated effort to reach God's intended destination for our life. *What does this take?* It requires that we understand the role the soul—our thoughts, will, and emotions—plays in making us more like Christ. Ultimately it's our responsibility to take charge of our soul by consciously, intentionally submitting it to God's Word, so that we might become healthier human beings, capable of doing His will.

> *When our journey becomes a quest, we want to expend a constant, conscious, concentrated effort to reach God's intended destination for our life.*

In the last decade I've come to see the extent to which Scripture and modern medical research on the mind/body/Spirit connection agree on the role our soul plays in promoting good health. I've applied mind/body/Spirit principles in my own life and used them in my professional practice, coming to realize they are natural partners in both physical healing and inner Sanctification. God's purposes, as revealed in Scripture, are our "compass settings." When we use our will, mind, and emotions to allow Him to navigate our souls in the direction of His purposes, we eventually arrive at them. Not doing so causes us to go off course, run ourselves aground, and leaves us stranded on the rocks—bailing! Actually, it is not our will alone, but *God working in us to will* and to do (Philippians 2:13). As Larry Osborne puts it:

> If I'm a genuine Christ follower, I have available within me the same Holy Spirit, who instructed, guided, and empowered Jesus and the early disciples. And that means my spiritual growth isn't so much the result of my hard work, intellect, and rigid self-discipline (all of which I could boast about). Instead, it's the direct result of my willingness to listen and yield to the Spirit's inner promptings as He works to guide and change me from the inside out. (excerpted from *Contrarian's Guide to Knowing God*)

Sanctification is a lifelong process that requires us to be willing to study God's Word, ask *Him* how we are to serve Him, and then obey His directions. We can't do that if we haphazardly drift along or insist on steering our own course instead of letting God take the helm.

Two

The Wrong Course
Resetting My Compass

"Commit your way to the Lord; trust in him and he will do this.
He will make your righteousness shine like the dawn."

—Psalm 37:5, 6

When we set out in the wrong direction, we're sure to run aground—no matter how *committed* we are to the course. Without correction, we'll end up on the rocks and shoals of outrageous circumstances we were never intended to encounter. I know all about running aground after setting out in the wrong direction. That was the story of my life for many years. A humorous story illustrates this power of *course correction*, and I'll share it here.

A sea captain named John found an unusual shipmate: a profane parrot. For some time, John had dreamed of having a special companion parrot to share with his crew that would help keep them happy and productive on long, lonely sea voyages. One day while ashore on an exotic trade island, John was offered a beautiful parrot named *Louise* who, amazingly, could speak English. The islanders warned John that although she was a beautiful and bright bird, Louise did have some problems. Grateful to have made such an extraordinary find, John took her as his own and promised he would always love and care for her—no matter what.

Once Louise was aboard, however, John discovered she had a bad attitude and an even worse vocabulary. She was rude, and her conversation was laced with profanity. John was deeply concerned. Louise's behavior could not possibly bring joy into the lives of his hard-working crew. He tried and tried to change the bird. He spoke only polite words in a soothing voice; he did everything else he could think of, but to no avail.

Finally John decided that Louise needed some "tough love." In a loud voice he demanded she clean up her act, but she just laughed and cursed louder than ever. Next he shook her. She just rustled her feathers and hissed at him. In desperation, John grabbed Louise and put her in the galley's freezer.

For a few minutes she squawked and kicked. Then suddenly there was total silence. Not a sound. Afraid he had hurt her, John threw open the freezer door. To his relief, Louise calmly stepped out onto his outstretched arm. "I believe I may have offended you," she said. "I'm sincerely sorry for my rude behavior and profane language. From this point on, I will behave respectfully and speak lovingly."

John couldn't believe his ears. Just as he was about to ask Louise what had caused her dramatic change, she hopped onto the edge of the freezer and peered inside. After a few moments, she looked back at John and said, "And what, may I ask, did the turkey do?"

FAITH IN THE WRONG COMPASS SETTING

Unlike Louise, I had to make more than one trip to the freezer before I got the message. I always believed that God was in my life, protecting me somehow, but I just didn't understand what Salvation or a personal relationship with God really *meant*. My mother taught me about "God," encouraged me to say my prayers every night, and always told me to "have faith." But my family didn't attend church, except on holidays. My mother told me early on she didn't want to cram religion down my throat and wanted me to decide on my own what I believed.

As young as age five, however, I had learned to doubt both God and myself. Up until that time, I had felt secure and safe. Suddenly everything changed. Under the influence of alcohol my father, began molesting me. The molestation, plus emotional abuse, contributed to the belief that I was an ugly, unintelligent, and generally worthless. I lost not only my sense of safety and security, but also my respect for the authority of all males, including God.

Although I called out to Him when desperate, I secretly wondered if God could actually hear me. In my dreams I would see the gentle faces of angels smiling down on me, and one night they seemed so real I thought I heard one say, "Shelley, no matter what happens, you will be all right. Just have faith." I believed them. I felt comforted.

My mother, a loving and wonderful woman, always told me the same thing when other kids would tease me about the sores on my body and face from eczema. But no comforting words from angels or my mother could rid me, at the time, of the feeling that God had betrayed me, nor restore my broken trust in Him.

Growing Up on the Wrong Course

When I became a teenager my life began to read like a certain chapter in an adolescent psychology text. You know the one. It says victims of early childhood molestation search endlessly for love…in all the wrong places. At age fourteen I became pregnant, and I chose to terminate the pregnancy in the only place available at the time, the back streets of Tijuana, Mexico.

I graduated from high school at seventeen and went

directly to college, but after one year, and doing poorly, I quit and went to work. At nineteen, I left the job and traveled for six months throughout Europe, playing my guitar and singing for food and lodging. I returned home and enrolled as a music major at the University of Southern California (USC). After two years the theatre arts department offered me an opportunity to perform in Europe. At the end of that stint, I decided to stay in England, during which time I wrote several songs, performing on stage and with the BBC. Then I spent a year in Norway before returning home to try my talents in Hollywood.

CONTINUING ON THE WRONG COURSE

Getting started in Hollywood was no easy task. I knew *no one* and had no money to live on until I got "discovered." I took waitress jobs and even briefly considered becoming a *Playboy*© bunny. At last I found an agent and began making inroads into Hollywood. I became a successful TV commercial actress and even got bit parts on the television series, *The Julie Andrews Show.*

During that time a showbiz girlfriend invited me to join a home Bible study hosted by Pat Boone and David Nelson, son of Ozzie and Harriet. Peace radiated from all those attending the home group. I sensed they had something *different* and extraordinary about them, but I failed to "get it," because my primary purpose for attending was to make "Hollywood" connections. I came for just two weeks.

Soon I was one of television's top five comedic commercial artists and was earning thousands of dollars a year on a single Listerine commercial. *Not bad for a thirty-one-year-old single female,* I thought.

At least I'd learned that I could be successful using my talents. But it wasn't enough. Feeling restless and unfulfilled, I auditioned as lead singer with a small music combo. We performed in a variety of performance venues and while performing at a funky bar in Kodiak, Alaska, I met a bright, attentive, and talented man. Six months later Mark and I were married.

My husband's childhood had been marked by poverty and abuse—and neither of us wanted children. We couldn't imagine why *anyone* would bring an innocent life into a world so filled with uncertainty, pain, and mistrust.

My husband worked as a commercial fisherman. Some months after we were married he returned home from an extended fishing trip and infected me with a highly contagious sexually transmitted disease (STD). Unbeknownst to me, though I was using precautionary measures, I conceived. The STD soon caused a severe infection and I became delirious, with a temperature of 105 degrees. Both the fetus and I were in jeopardy, my physician said. He encouraged a therapeutic abortion which, sadly, helped to rationalize yet another pregnancy termination. At the time, pro-life advocates were picketing the clinic. My guilt and self-hatred increased tenfold. Several months later I was told that my chances for a safe or viable pregnancy in the future were unlikely because of the residual scarring of the infection. I would never have children.

It wasn't an easy time in other ways, either. My husband fished year-round and would be gone for several months at a time. We lived on isolated islands in Alaska, far away from family and friends. Fortunately, I found companionship and new life interests among the friendly and productive people who lived there. Over time I became a state certified public safety officer, a firefighter, and an emergency medical technician. In 1982, I was accepted into the Health Sciences Program at the University of Washington in Seattle for postgraduate certification as a physician assistant in family medicine. In that same year, my mother died of cancer.

Although I was very successful in medical school, at thirty-nine years old my life was spiraling downward. After the pregnancy termination, my husband's angry outbursts further decreased my ability to trust. My desire to flee from an abusive marriage, the death of my beloved mother, and a growing self-hatred led to a near fatal relapse of *eosinophilic gastroenteritis* (EG), a lifelong, chronic autoimmune illness that would remain undiagnosed until age forty-two. These multiple psychological stressors were causing a near-death scenario from the out-of-control physical reactions of total body eczema, asthma, hay fever, migraines, and severe intestinal complications. This was a classic mind/body connection, but without the hope of the Spirit.

During my illness I spent time with a special childhood friend and her husband, mature and strong Christians who prayed over me. They gave me hope that I could trust God and I began my very slow journey toward a personal relationship with Jesus Christ.

Up until this time I had practiced what I *thought* was faith. I thought I knew what it was to believe in God. I just couldn't really trust Him. When things got tough I would pray that everything would be all right, and things always got better. But eventually I would find myself back in a crisis, either with my health or in my relationships. What I didn't know was that God loved and protected me, despite my mistrust of Him, and that He had a specific purpose in mind just for me. The next twenty years would be a testimony to His patient and loving refinement in my life.

Still married, I returned to Alaska. Although I was still quite frail and thin, my symptoms were under control. So, now that I was a physician's assistant, I volunteered at the local family clinic, just to keep busy while my husband was at sea. Eight hundred air miles from the nearest hospital in

Anchorage, this small island clinic had only one physician and one nurse. They were happy to have me.

I began working alongside Ken, a kind, quiet Christian doctor who'd arrived a year earlier. We frequently pulled ten to eighteen hour shifts. After weeks of working so closely, we developed a sense of trust and safety with each other, and unwisely began to share our feelings about the severe challenges in our marriages. In my eleven years of marriage, and in his twenty-five, neither of us had talked with anyone about our circumstances, and neither of us had ever been unfaithful.

Over time we fell in love and had an affair. Our actions were unconscionable and immoral, and we both knew it. We were mortified and ashamed. As a minister's son, Ken agonized over how deeply he had disappointed and hurt God, his family, and his parents. With both my parents deceased, there was no one to reference in this way. I simply realized I had sinned against God and my husband. Never in our lives had we known such suffering. Determined to do the right thing, I said goodbye and moved back to Anchorage, knowing I could never see Ken again.

What I didn't know was that God loved and protected me, despite my mistrust of Him, and that He had a specific purpose in mind just for me.

Changing Course

I wanted to do what was right for my marriage and for myself, so I began counseling with a therapist. When my husband's physical and psychological abuse escalated, I filed for divorce. Mark became very distraught and begged me to meet him in a private hotel room so we could talk over my decision. Knowing his temper, I was worried about meeting alone with him, but I decided to go. When I arrived he was sitting on the side of one of the beds; I sat down across from him on the other. I still wasn't totally recovered from the effects of the eosinophilic gastroenteritis (EG) and I tired easily. All I really wanted to do right then was to lie down and sleep.

I remained attentive while he pleaded for us to stay married. His sorrow ripped through my soul. But I knew that if I stayed I would not survive. I said nothing while I struggled to find caring words. My silence infuriated him. Suddenly he reached down into his sea bag and pulled out a loaded .357 magnum and pointed it at my head. With shaking hands and voice he said, "If I can't have you, Shelley, nobody will!"

I realized that no matter what I said, if he meant to shoot me, there was nothing I could say or do to stop him. A part of me even *welcomed* the idea of putting an end to my guilt and shame-filled existence. Yet the immediate effect of his threat was to plunge me deeper into fatigue. It took tremendous control just to keep my eyelids from clamping shut. I quickly prayed to God, asking for strength and wisdom. A moment later, I prayed silently, looked directly into his distorted face, and said calmly, "I know I can't control what you do to me, but I am so tired. I don't have enough strength to talk with you right now. I need to sleep. If you are really going to shoot me, please find it in your heart to wait until I am asleep." That said, I lay down and immediately slipped out of consciousness, into an oblivious slumber.

Forty-five minutes later I awoke to find my husband still sitting opposite me. His head and shoulders were slumped, and his hands, still grasping the gun, were pointed toward the floor. When I opened my eyes, he glanced over. Our eyes locked. My stomach churned, and I silently prayed again, "*God, help me*," but said nothing. He sat there for a moment, and then put the gun back into his duffle bag, picked up his things, and slowly walked out of the room, closing the door gently behind him. The divorce became final.

Four months later Mark married a mutual friend whose husband had been killed in an automobile accident six months earlier. Though my ship had veered *way* off in the wrong direction, God was still watching over me, hearing my prayers to Him, and gently correcting my course.

Three

The Great Rescue

A New Course

"The Lord God formed the man from the dust of the ground and breathed into his nostrils the breath of life, and the man became a living being."

—Genesis 2:7

Genesis 1:27 says God created us "in His own image." So, when God created us in the culminating act of Creation, He gave mankind a body, a soul, and a spirit. God *is Spirit,* and He made *us* part spirit so that we could interact with Him in spirit, as well. Reflecting His own nature, which contains the capacity to think, to feel, and to exercise free will, God gave each of us a soul. Our *soul* is the part of our being that thinks, feels, and decides on a course of action.

Shipwrecked

At Creation, all three parts of our God-given nature—*body, soul, and spirit*—were in perfect harmony. God had created us to live forever, and our spirits were perfectly attuned to Him. Adam's soul was in complete agreement with God's thoughts, feelings, and will. His body happily followed the decisions of his soul. However, all this changed when our first parents chose to rebel against God.

With the Fall of Man, mankind died spiritually, and physical death would be the eventual, inevitable result. Our intellect was darkened, our will debilitated, and our feelings were corrupted. Our soul inclined away from God, and leaned toward self. It became a "fallen nature." (The Bible also calls this nature the "old man" or "sin nature.") Our soul sought to *do its own thing* rather than God's will. Our once-immortal human body now became subject to suffering, disease, decay, and death. Because of this, our bodies, feelings, and wills would be born in need of restoration and healing.

But God loved us too much to leave us in this soul-shipwrecked condition! He sent His beloved Son, Jesus Christ, to earth to pay the penalty of death for sin, thus to release *us* from the death penalty. Some think Jesus Christ did this just to rescue our *soul* from death and destruction, but He did it to rescue our *body* and our *spirit,* as well.

The body is important to God; he wants us to be well. 3 John 1:2 says:

> Beloved, I wish above all things that thou mayest prosper and be in health, even as thy soul prospereth. (KJV)

Christ was born with a body, was crucified in a body, and was resurrected in a *heavenly body*. He will live in a heavenly body forever, and ultimately all those who accept God's Son as the redeeming Sacrifice for sin will live in heavenly bodies, as well. Most believers have a story about how God "corrected their course" and guided them into the knowledge of Christ. Mine begins here....

A NEW COURSE

When I was nearly four years old my family attended a special Christmas service at a large church in Los Angeles. The choir sat in a balcony above the congregation, hidden from view. As soon as they began singing, a wonderful sensation came over me. For the first time in my short life, I experienced total body *gooseflesh*. Never had I heard such beautiful sounds! I looked around, trying to figure out where the transporting music was coming from. Seeing nothing, I nudged my mother and whispered, "Mama, are we in heaven?"

I soon discovered God had gifted me with a voice for singing, and I joined the church choir. My parents would attend service when I sang solos. I also went to Sunday school. That goosebump reaction frequently returned when I sang in church or heard the Word of God.

I would have to wait until age thirty-one, however, for the gospel of Salvation to be shared with me personally by a lifelong friend. That's when I finally heard and *believed* God's message of forgiveness, hope, and healing. My Salvation was a once-and-for-all event in which God renewed my spirit so that I could have uninterrupted fellowship with Him, just as Adam and Eve had enjoyed before their fall from grace, which was caused by their choice to disobey God, or *sin. Just what is sin,* anyway?

After I was saved I learned from Christian teachers that sinning means *falling short of God's standard of perfect rightness,* or righteousness. To "sin" is an archery term, one that indicates the arrows we've shot have hit way short—*or right or left*—of the intended target: the perfect bull's-eye. Nevertheless, when I prayed for forgiveness for my sins, I learned, Scripture promised that in God's eyes I was now *spiritually* perfect. By my faith in Jesus' perfect offering of Himself to "pay for my sins," when God looked at me now, He saw what I was to become in His Son. (That's the same gift He offers to everyone who will receive it.) The word *perfect,* I learned, refers to our *position* with God. The word in original Greek means *complete*. In Christ our spirit, soul, and body are fully integrated. In other words, we are "justified" in God's sight. When converted, it is just as if we had *never sinned*.

When I received Christ I knew immediately that God had made me spiritually alive and, for a time, my life improved greatly. My faith deepened and my self-acceptance grew. I had Someone who cared about me who would watch over me forever!

SAME OL' PILOT

For many years I thought that was all there was to it. Although I was saved, I kept relying on the same old methods of getting things done. I thought I needed to be at the ship's helm, and I took whatever course required the least effort to reach the goals I set for myself. As a result, I continued to run aground. Because of my continuing ignorance and arrogance, and insistence on being at the helm, I suffered an abusive first marriage, an infidelity, divorce, major surgeries, and some near-death experiences. God used each experience to mature and attract me to seek Him, but I knew He wanted to do more than just prove His love by rescuing me off rocky shoals time after time.

What I didn't understand was *my* part of the deal. I was a sincere and believing Christian, but I had yet to appreciate the missing piece in my Christian walk. Without that piece I would never truly understand God's greater purpose for my life. About ten years ago, in the midst of a near-death experience from a ruptured colon, the fusion of my cervical spine, and metastatic cancer, I sensed I was missing an essential piece in my Christian faith. This left me feeling fearful and frustrated.

I think many Christians experience this same thing after Salvation. Jason, a new believer, came to see me feeling deeply discouraged and depressed. He shared that he earnestly believed in, trusted, and loved Christ. He knew that God wanted him not only to experience the love He had for him, but also to know what it means to truly love himself and others. Yet Jason was not experiencing love on the human level, and so he was unhappy and confused. He couldn't understand why, as a true believer, he couldn't get along better with his family and friends. He quoted 2 Corinthians 5:17: "If anyone is in Christ, he is a new creation; the old has gone, the new has come!" He *knew* he was a new creation, but for some reason he didn't *feel* so new.

It was the same for me. When I came to see how often God had spared me in distresses my desire to truly know Him as my Lord began to grow. But in all I set out to do and accomplish, the negative evaluation of myself remained. On the outside it appeared I was a real success in life. But, in my mind, I was still an ugly, stupid, unlovable little girl. No matter what I accomplished, these thoughts kept me from opening my eyes and ears to Him. It all boiled down to the fact that I didn't understand the process of Sanctification, or progressive maturity. I didn't realize that until I changed my self-focused *victim* stance to that of a God-focused *victor*, I could not properly understand or respond to God's divine promptings and purpose for my life.

I thought most outcomes in life were related to my belief that I was in charge and I would succeed or fail based on my intelligence, my gifts, and my hard work. In other words, everything was usually all about *me*. I didn't yet know what it truly meant to participate cooperatively in the Sanctification process. I think the reason many of my counseling clients come to see me is that they don't yet comprehend this, either.

> *Until I changed my self-focused* victim *stance to that of a God-focused* victor, *I could not properly understand or respond to God's divine promptings and purpose for my life.*

OLD MAN OVERBOARD

When Jesus went back to the Father He sent His Spirit to dwell within our hearts. The Holy Spirit's job is to make us more like Christ, not only by *reviving* our carnal, dead spirit so we can once again commune with God, but also by *restoring* our soul—so that we can agree with God. He "tunes" our free will, harmonizing it with God's will. This energizes our bodies and minds so that we can carry out His will on Earth.

Through the work of the Holy Spirit in us we are progressively being helped to become more like Jesus. This is what *Sanctification* is all about. It's a lifelong process that begins by our recognizing God's right to direct our life and agreeing to cooperate with *His* plan. Once we do that, God progressively reveals the course He has charted specifically for us as we carry out our part of His Kingdom-agenda on earth.

This sanctifying process requires our cooperation and only truly begins when, by faith, in gratitude to God, we offer ourselves—*body, soul, and spirit*—to Him to do with us as He chooses (Romans 12:1). It takes some a long time and lots of trouble before we become willing to do this. We have to throw our old man, our old self, overboard before we'll relinquish control and let God grow a new nature in us. It seems most of us wait until we are sinking beneath surging waves before we ask for help or let go of our own plans and determine to follow His. This answers the age-old, frequently asked question: "Why does God allow problems and difficulties to come into our lives?"

Others went out on the sea in ships…they saw the works of the Lord, His wonderful deeds in the deep… He spoke and stirred up a tempest… their courage melted away and they were at their wit's end…they cried out to the Lord in their trouble and He brought them out of their distress. He stilled the storm to a whisper and he guided them to their desired haven. (Psalm 107:23–30)

Once we cooperate with the Holy Spirit by choosing to surrender to God, Jason's reference to 2 Corinthians 5:17 starts to make sense. Scripture says, "…if anyone is in Christ, he is a new creation; the old has gone, the new has come." Gradually, God begins to change our desires on a deeper level so they align more closely with His own. We begin to think God's thoughts in our minds, feel His feelings in our hearts, and choose to use our bodies in ways that are pleasing to Him. The Holy Spirit gives us the desire to obey God and the power to do what pleases Him. Now we are truly being sanctified and, "the old has gone, the new has come!"

It took me many years to begin cooperating with God, but when I finally did, the benefits of the "new" started coming right away. The whole world began to open up to me:

- My counseling practice grew and my ministry expanded.
- *The Sampler*, my first book, was published.
- I was given opportunities for television and radio interviews.
- I was on the road one week of every month giving my testimony.
- A Christian college invited me to become an adjunct faculty member.
- Requests for giving weekend retreats arrived from in and out of state.

There was no doubt in my mind that God was giving me these opportunities to serve Him and to love others. I began to forgive and love myself, even as He loved me.

At the point we decide to stay *God's course* no matter what, our Christian journey becomes a quest toward progressively becoming more like Jesus and using our life to love and serve God and others. Though storms will come, we have God's assurance we will never sink beneath the waves—though we may sometimes *feel* like we're drowning. With Jesus as our firm anchor, in times of turbulence we will simply circle close to Him until the wind changes.

FOUR

An Anchor for the Soul

Behaviors Are Tied to Thoughts

*"We have this hope as an anchor for the soul,
firm and secure...."*

—HEBREWS 6:19

In the Sanctification process that follows the act of believing, the Holy Spirit begins to heal your mind and emotions so you can exercise free will and choose to live life God's way. Your part is to *allow* Him to do that—to be *willing to be made willing*—instead of resisting growth and change. Little by little, as you cooperate with God, He then cuts away the *dead weight* that holds you motionless in your pursuit of Sanctification, health, and wellbeing.

DRAGGING ANCHOR

An anchor can make you secure or it can drag you down. We each have our habits of thinking that keep us from knowing and acting on the truth. One of mine was *false humility*. Pride, masquerading as humility, has dragged me down on many occasions in my life, and it was an anchor God had to cut loose before I could get my relationship with Him underway.

As a new author I worried about how many books I could or *should* be selling. I felt stressed, scared, and otherwise focused on myself and worldly outcomes for the publication. One day during a session with my media coach I began complaining about how hard it was to feel confident as I tried to sell my book to so many listeners. He called me up short on it.

"If your focus is on selling the book instead of on sharing God's message, Shelley, how can you possibly hear what God has planned for you?" he asked. "You need to understand it's not about you. It's about being confident that your true desire is to spread God's message of forgiveness, hope, and healing. He will provide for your needs. Let Him decide where and how to use the book and you'll discover *His* purpose for it."

Kyle encouraged me to change my tendency to think I was inadequate and people were just waiting to judge me. He told me that while God doesn't always invite the qualified, He always qualifies those whom He's invited. I needed to understand that God's plan to use me for His glory wasn't *about* me. An abundant life for His Glory was certainly His intention *for* me. I got the message. I began to think about what God was planning for my life. I no longer focused on selling books. Instead, I focused on waiting for God to show me how, when, and where He wanted me to speak His message. I finally understood my responsibility to stop, wait, and listen for God. In other words, I chose God to be my anchor. When you do this you stabilize, and you're no longer dragged down in the whirlpool of self-focus.

Right now you might be thinking, *Wait a minute! This is just who I am. Trying to change what makes me tick would be like trying to change the color of my eyes.* But Sanctification is not about changing the nature of your *being*. It's about changing the nature of your *behavior*, and this begins with the mind.

Paul's writings reveal a great deal about the mind/body/Spirit connection and its relation to Sanctification.

> So here's what I want you to do, God helping you: take your every day, ordinary life—your sleeping, eating, going to work, and walking around life—and place it before God as an offering. Embracing what God does for you is the best thing you can do for Him. (Romans 12:1, *The Message*)

Now, you may be wondering: *How am I supposed to do that?*

If you wish to bring your soul, your body, and your spirit into harmony, you must begin by disciplining your mind. Choosing to do so will, in time, change both your behavior and your feelings, making you progressively more like Christ.

> *It's not about changing the nature of your being.*
> *It's about changing the nature of your behavior,*
> *and this begins with the mind.*

There are several neurological principles that can help us understand the workings of the mind. One is that once our subconscious mind has accepted an idea, it remains unchanged until another idea takes its place. The longer an idea is held, the more it becomes a habit of thinking, which is how habits of action, whether healthy or not, are formed. First there is a thought, then a feeling, then a decision, and then an action.

If we are to step out into the life God has for us it is *imperative* we change our thinking. If we hold onto thoughts that have resulted from disappointing, wounding experiences, or from not believing in God's forgiveness, then these negative perceptions become lies that can deafen our ears to hear God's plan for us or open us up to temptation.

WAVES OF DEAFENING THOUGHTS

As a singer and actress I performed on stage for many years. In all that time a very trusted, older friend of mine managed to attend nearly every production, including some in Alaska and in Europe. She was always an inspiration to me because I considered her to be a strong and intelligent woman who seemed to have conquered her fears and accomplished everything she'd set out to do in life. She always encouraged me to do the same, and I suppose she gave me the courage to do it, even though inside I felt incapable and inadequate to confidently achieve anything.

When at last I understood I had to change my thoughts about myself I wanted to share God's message of Salvation and love with my friend. She was experiencing destructive changes in her life and was still relying on her own strength, but her words and actions told me she was afraid. Understandably angry at the prospect of losing her independence and the comfortable life she had known, she was uncooperative with her immediate family and friends, who wanted very much to help her. I knew if she would turn to Jesus and rely on Him she would have an anchor for her soul and a peace she had never known. I told her how God had changed my life, knowing she could see that *something* in my life had shifted. Though she thought this was *all very nice* for me, she clung to her self-focused worldview and angry, fearful thoughts.

When my speaking tour reached my old friend's city, I asked if she would like to come hear my testimony. I wanted her to understand why my life and countenance had changed so radically. She came, and when it was my time to speak, she seemed to be listening intently. My heart leapt for joy.

At the end of my testimony I saw my friend jump up and head for the door, managing to meet her there just before she exited. She was very loving and gave me a big hug. As we looked into each other's eyes, she said, "Shelley, of all the performances I have watched you give, this was by far the best. And you had no costume, no orchestra, no stage or set design. You were just wonderful!" With that, she scooted out the door.

I stood there with tears welling up in my eyes. She loved me and truly meant well, but didn't she know? This was the first time she had ever seen me in front of a group of people when I *wasn't* performing. What she actually saw was a woman whose ideas and purpose in life were being radically transformed. After years of resisting the notion that God loved me and wanted to use me to glorify Himself, His truth was finally setting me free to follow His plan for my life. But my friend, trapped in her fearful thinking, as *I* had once also been, was deaf to God's call.

DEATH-DEALING HABITS ANCHORED IN THE MIND

My friend's reaction illustrates another important principle and truth about the mind: The longer an old, flawed idea remains, the more opposition there is to replacing it with a new, healthier idea. A simple way to understand this statement is to think again about our habits.

Have you ever tried to break a bad habit? The desire to make New Year's resolutions never dies, but our will to see them through usually does. *Why?* It's very challenging to change a belief—and a resulting behavior—once it has found its way into the deep recesses of your mind. Simply put, it's just easier *not* to change.

The longer a negative habit continues unbroken or unchanged, the easier it is to hang on to it. Once a death-dealing habit is anchored in the mind, it becomes difficult to break. The way to change that habit is first to *make a decision* to do so. Then, suggest to yourself a life-enhancing thought and *act on it* in order to replace the old behavior. To be most effective, we need to do this repeatedly over a period of at least thirty days. The more often we do this, the less of a tendency there will be to revert back to the negative habit. Once the subconscious mind accepts the new idea and acts on it, the more ingrained it will become.

I have seen this principle at work in the life of a dear friend. Years ago she came to see me because she experienced intense stage fright. She was an accomplished dancer. However, deep inside she thought she was never good enough. Because her performances were only about audience approval and supporting her own feelings of low self-worth, her performance anxiety was so high she vomited before each and every performance. No matter how well she understood the underlying psychological implications her thoughts never changed, so neither did the symptoms.

Then, about two years ago, she called to tell me how her new life with Christ had set her free by helping her change her thoughts. She recognized the need to replace the negative image she'd created for herself by using Scripture to affirm God's positive image of her instead. Why, she wondered, hadn't I given her that perspective and resource years ago when I spoke of my faith in God and how He had helped me? The answer is that at the time, I didn't *know* those truths, nor did I *apply* them in a personal way. Now we both rejoice knowing the power He has to change our lives as He helps us change our thoughts and behaviors.

When you decide to start changing your thoughts, begin with simple, doable suggestions for new, life-enhancing behavior. Once you are rewarded with a positive experience, build that new habit by suggesting the thought again. Your mind will recognize the message and send it throughout your body. The more your body recognizes the reward, the more it will be willing to continue.

Remember, changing our negative behaviors sometimes will have less to do with *relearning* new habits than *unlearning* the old ones. Both are required. That's the challenge.

I'm sure you've heard the old saying, "Practice makes perfect." It might be more accurate to say, "Practicing perfection makes perfect," along with, "Practice makes permanent." So, it's imperative to make sure you're practicing the right things—the truths of God's Word—on a continuous basis. At first this may be uncomfortable, and it will definitely require effort. Yet the habit of *choosing correct thinking* is paramount to experiencing Sanctification in your life. Remember: this "practice of perfection" is the act of affirming God's truth about you, not an exercise of mind over matter. It is doing your soul's part, in cooperation with the Holy Spirit, to bring your will into harmony with and conformity to the perfect will of God.

FIVE

Taking the Wind out of Fear's Sails

With God, All Things are Possible

> *"God is our refuge and strength,*
> *an ever-present help in trouble.*
> *Therefore we will not fear...."*
>
> —PSALMS 46:1, 2

The energy of positive or negative thoughts is like wind—or *no wind*—to a ship's sails. Without wind, we go nowhere, yet our sails must be properly set for our ship to move forward. Because our thoughts and will lie in the sector of the soul, the *soul factor* lets us cooperate with God in our Sanctification and healing. When we intentionally set our sails (thoughts and will) to the course God holds for our lives, we achieve the mind/body/Spirit connection and move forward.

The existence of this connection has been a controversial subject. Hippocrates, the ancient Greek "father of medicine," taught that the soul and the body should be treated as a whole. Western medicine, however, is based on the belief that the soul and body are largely unrelated, since the body is subject to physical laws, but the soul is not. The radical difference between these beliefs results in very different conclusions about *how we heal* and thus how we should medically treat both physical and mental illness.

Navigating Toward Health

Long before the first glimmerings of modern science, Scripture taught us that the way people think and feel—the *condition of the soul*—has a strong influence on the body. Indeed:

> As a man thinks in his heart, so is he. (Proverbs 23:7)

Certainly, our thoughts are inextricably linked to *who we really are*. When Rene Descartes, esteemed 17th century French philosopher and mathematician, did an exhaustive search for physical proof to demonstrate that the soul and body are connected, he could find no measurable evidence. His powerful influence over the medical community of his day gave rise to the *mechanistic* approach to modern medicine. Comparable to a ship mechanic's analysis of an engine malfunction as a system of parts that needs to be repaired, it looks at human illness, malfunction, and breakdown as mechanical "systems failures."

Hippocrates said the great error of his day was that, "...the physicians separate the soul from the body." Those who agree will conclude that knowing what's going on in a patient's mind when distressing physical symptoms are present is essential to deciding what course of treatment to follow. On the other hand, those who adhere to the mainstream Western or *traditional* view that germs or physical (parts) breakdowns cause disease will frequently focus on symptoms and prescribe a particular medicine to eradicate them.

Fortunately there have always been Western medical researchers and practitioners who've resisted the notion that physical treatment is the *only* way to approach the healing process. Since the nineteenth century, studies on the impact of the mind on the central nervous system and the effects of stress on the endocrine and immune systems have now proven there is a chemical connection between the state of our soul and the condition of our body.

Scientists once believed those chemical messenger molecules known as *neuropeptides* existed only in the brain, which sent them out in response to a problem in some part of the body. Now we know that *peptides* are everywhere.

They carry messages within the brain, from the brain to the body, from the body to the brain, and from body parts to parts throughout the body. As these messengers travel they provide vital, almost *instantaneous* communication of information. As Scripture has always taught, the mind and body are profoundly interdependent.

Though the connection between the soul and body has been self-evident since creation, only during the past forty years has scientific study empirically demonstrated the correlation between psychological stress and common health challenges such as high blood pressure, headaches, ulcers, depression, asthma, and autoimmune disorders like allergies and some types of arthritis.

Simply defined, *stress* is an individual response to an internal or external demand. It starts in two major body systems: the nervous system and the endocrine system. Our nervous system responds nearly instantaneously to a perceived threat. This is called the *fight or flight* response. The endocrine system consists of more than two hundred hormones secreted by the brain, pancreas, ovaries, testes, adrenal, thyroid, and other key glands. These powerful hormonal responses take longer to kick in, but once they start flowing, the effects last much longer. If not relieved by bringing the body back into a state of equilibrium, disease may begin or an existing condition may worsen.

CLINGING TO A LIFE PRESERVER

The extent to which symptoms manifest in our bodies is directly related to the extent of unresolved stress in our lives. I know how stress played an important role in the status of eosinophilic gastroenteritis (EG) in my life. During my medical training in the early 1980s I began to understand the correlation of stress with illness and to realize my mind could impact my body in a *negative* or a *positive* way. As a means of relief from debilitating symptoms, I began to study the mind/body connection. Nevertheless, right after I finished postgraduate medical studies, the circumstances of my life became so stressful they overwhelmed my body. I had just lost my mother to cancer, my marriage was failing, and I was only now beginning to deal with the impact of early childhood molestation and family alcoholism. Unable to cope, I lost even my desire to live and became critically ill with a relapse of the autoimmune disease.

I became extremely sensitive to all foods, environmental odors, and even the medications that had previously given me relief. My weight plummeted, my hair fell out, my skin was covered from head to toe with weeping lesions, and my breathing was labored. No one knew what was happening to my body, nor *why*.

Having exhausted traditional medical approaches, as a

last resort I went to see a Christian counselor who practiced a Christ-focused technique that gave me the opportunity to revisit events from my past that had negatively affected my self-perception. The counselor was a godly woman and a highly qualified therapist. I was skeptical, but I figured I had nothing to lose.

During the first sessions my mind returned to places from my early childhood. My breathing became labored, my skin itched, and I developed hives. I started scratching and crying. Although I didn't quite get it at the time, that was the first real demonstration to me that my thoughts could cause a powerful physical response. It was a lifesaving breakthrough of understanding for me. I came to understand that the thoughts I entertained could either enhance or hamper my physical health.

Hippocrates had said, "Health depends on a state of equilibrium among the various factors that govern the operation of the body and the mind; the equilibrium, in turn, is reached only when man lives in harmony with his external environment" (*Geoffrey Purves, Healthy Living Centres: A Guide to Primary Health Care Designs*). But living in a state of equilibrium and harmony with our environment is a choice of the will. It requires thought and effort, and this is the real *work* of the soul. It is most effectively achieved when we cooperate with the soul-prompting influence of the Holy Spirit in our lives.

Shelter from the Storm

One particular study that deepened my understanding of the mind/body connection was a National Institute of Health (NIH) study in which researchers used *psychological desensitizing* techniques to increase levels of the white cells that fight disease (*lymphocytes*). These have been proven to decrease under stress.

A woman in the study was terrified of snakes. When she entered the clinic in which she hoped to find relief from this phobia, she was unable to stand even twelve feet from a *picture* of snakes. Noting the woman's terrified response to the picture, researchers drew blood from her and measured her white blood cell count, which had decreased. Then, over a period of a few days, she applied a method of relaxation techniques, prayer, and a mindset of victory to reduce her fear of snakes.

When this process was complete she was seated before a table, directly in front of a large glass terrarium. A boa constrictor was slithering around behind the glass, yet she was able to sit calmly. She even put her hands on each side of the container while they measured her blood pressure. It was normal. They also measured her white blood cell count again. It had risen by an astonishing twenty-five percent!

Since my own medical training was primarily in the health sciences, it was exciting for me to see, given new advances in technology, that the mind/body/ Spirit connection can now be demonstrated and measured in the above ways. For medical science to be able to observe it under a microscope is evidence to me of God's complex mechanism to provide the greatest potential for the healing of all parts of our being.

This study taught me that when we are willing to do the necessary *soul work* by changing our thoughts, we can also change our emotions and the physical state of our body. When we think rationally, fear is potentially lifesaving because it prepares us for *fight* or *flight*. When our fears are irrational, however, they ultimately cause psychological stress, which in turn depresses the ability of our immune system to fight off disease—and sometimes sets us up to behave in ways that are self-destructive.

In the Bible, God tells us 365 times *not to fear*—one reminder for each day of the year. Clearly, God does not intend for us to live in fear, for fear is an emotion that puts great stress on the body. In His mercy, He has revealed just how fear impacts our body and how the mind/body/Spirit connection can keep fear from harming us.

Propelled by Fear

Irrational fear not only has the potential to harm your body—it can also slow the Sanctification process by keeping you from doing what you know God wants you to do. You may *know* God wants you to do something, but fear you're not able to accomplish His purposes. Gideon felt frightened, with good cause, when God asked him to reduce his fighting force against a strong enemy from 32,000 to 300 warriors. In response to Gideon's fear, God said, "Go in the strength you have...I am sending you" (Judges 6:14). Start with what God has already given you, then move forward, and you will see His purposes fulfilled. As you step out in faith, the Holy Spirit makes His help and presence known—filling your sails with His wind and His steady power source!

> *Irrational fear can also slow the Sanctification process by keeping you from doing what you know God wants you to do.*

It took me a while to learn this principle. When God called me to write *The Sampler*, I felt incapable of writing well enough to adequately express God's message. I had a deep-seated fear that writing down my thoughts would show everybody how incompetent I was. On one hand, I knew God was leading me to write about what He'd done in my life but, on the other hand I wondered: *Why in the world would He want me to do this? I can't do it!*

My dear editor, Judith, asked me to consider how Moses had tried to use his speech impediment with God as an excuse to turn down the mission God was calling him to fulfill: lead the Israelites out of slavery in Egypt. After asking God to please *send somebody else,* God told him he would send his brother, Aaron, to help him to speak to Pharoah. Despite his fear, Moses finally accepted the calling, aligning his thoughts and will with the will of God.

If God wants us to do something, as He did Gideon and Moses, He will send us everything and everyone we need to help us accomplish it. He is our strength—and He often helps us through other people. If that weren't true, I would still be talking about, rather than writing about, the difference it can make when we cooperate with the Holy Spirit by *turning our sails,* or changing our thinking to align with God's own.

"Row, Row, Row Your Boat"

Twenty years ago I learned about that difference and experienced the mind/body/Spirit connection in an *up close and personal* way. After my divorce from Mark, I found a job at the Alaska Native Medical Center, where I taught primary medicine to Native Americans, who would then take their training back to assist the populations of remote Alaskan villages. A year passed. My friend Ken and his wife had been in marital counseling, yet had separated. In 1988, a year after they divorced, Ken and I were married.

Shortly after our wedding Ken and I went cross-country skiing in sub-zero weather at Sheep Mountain Resort in Alaska. As we approached a steep ridge known as "Thriller," the extreme cold and physical exertion produced in me the first signs of bronchial constriction. I'd forgotten to use my inhaler before we set out, and had not brought it with me, either. This created a critical, emergency situation.

We were about forty-five minutes from the main lodge if we backtracked, and twenty minutes away if we headed up *Thriller.* Time was of the essence. No one else was on the trail. There was no way Ken could carry or even *pull* me back to the lodge. There was only one thing I could do besides pray—which I'd already begun to do, fervently!

Because of my long history with autoimmune challenges I had investigated through the years several ways to relieve my symptoms, in addition to taking medicines. One of the most helpful interventions I'd learned was to draw on my mind's thoughts to mitigate the physiological impact of assaults on my body. I now began to use what I'd learned about the power of healthy words on my bodily functions to open my lumen (the large and small air tubes in my lungs.)

Though I was still able to get some air in, despite my best mental efforts, exhaling was becoming more and more of a challenge. I felt fearful and started to panic as my body struggled to get oxygen *into* and carbon dioxide *out of* my brain cells and body. My lips were getting numb and my fingers were tingling. I was losing the ability to focus my mind.

"Ken, talk to my body," I said in a slurred voice. "Help me breathe."

Aware of the power of suggestion, he told me I was relaxing my body, thereby enabling air to flow easily both in and out of my lungs. We both prayed. After several minutes of prayer and allowing his words to seep into my mind, I felt better and suggested we slowly start the twenty-minute ascent up *Thriller*. Once we reached the top, it would take only five minutes to arrive at our cabin and my inhaler.

Starting off together, I made up my own version of "Row, Row, Row Your Boat" to get me up the steep slope. I started to sing silently: "Row, row, row your boat, gently down my lumen. Merrily, merrily, merrily, merrily, see my lumen open." We reached the top and skied down. By the time we got to the cabin, I was breathing normally.

Two years after our Sheep Mountain adventure, while Ken and I were vacationing at the Oregon coast, I had another serious asthma attack. We had just finished dining with some of our friends at a popular seafood restaurant. They'd decided to share tidbits from each entrée. Aware of how allergic I am to crab meat, I nibbled selectively. As careful as I was, however, I must have ingested a small amount of crab somehow.

Shortly after Ken and I returned to our campsite my tongue and lips began to tingle and itch; my breathing became labored. We both recognized the first telltale signs of anaphylactic shock. The first medical intervention should be a quick-acting inhaler followed, if needed, by an injection of epinephrine. But since the asthma had been mostly under control since Sheep Mountain, I had neglected to pack my inhaler before we left on our trip.

Ken was eager to get me to the emergency room, but my memories of Sheep Mountain prompted me to say, "Let's do some prayer and have you talk to my lungs first. I want to give God a chance. He helped before. Talk to my lungs, honey," I said.

With my eyes shut, I pictured Jesus sitting next to me as I silently began to sing, "Row, row, row Your boat, gently down my lumen...."

Ken helped me lean my back against his knees and started speaking to my body. He continued on for several minutes, until I felt my breathing start to relax. I leaned forward, slowly got up, and asked him to help me get to the nearby clubhouse for a hot shower. Years earlier, while I was learning to stand vigil over my body, I'd discovered that hot showers would bring at least twenty minutes of relief from incessant itching.

Now Ken grabbed a towel and we made our way over to the women's shower area. I undressed and allowed the healing, calming effects of the water to rush over me. I felt my body and lungs relax with every breath I took. I meditated on Christ, as though I were perfectly well and breathing easily, while silently continuing to sing my little song. To me, these intentional actions were "setting my sails to the wind," as I waited on the Holy Spirit to fill me, heal me, and move me forward.

After forty-five minutes I turned off the water and got dressed. Ken and I walked back to the trailer together in silence. Before we went to bed, we thanked God for His healing power. I slept soundly for a few hours, leaning against Ken, and when I awoke my breathing had been completely restored.

Six

Sunken Treasure
Focusing on God Fills My Heart

"Where your treasure is, there will your heart be also."

— MATTHEW 6:21

The mind/body/Spirit connection explains why our thoughts—and, by extension, our words—can affect the body so dramatically. When an asthma attack occurs, for instance, we naturally become anxious. Anxiety causes our brain to secrete certain *neurotransmitters,* which in turn cause the bronchi (tubes in our lungs) to constrict even more. This makes the asthma worse, and makes us *more* anxious, forming a vicious cycle. If we remain anxious for a long period of time, medical science predicts the long-term effects of chronic stress can trigger physical illnesses like cancer and heart disease.

Hook, Line and Sinker

I'm not sure why a diagnosis of depression, anxiety, or even physical illness can generate feelings of guilt and shame in many of us. I *do* know guilt and shame cause damage, however, since these two have been deeply disturbing even to me at times.

Christians are sometimes told that if we would only *pray harder* or *correct the sin* in our lives, we would not experience sickness at all. We tend to buy these heavy admonishments hook, line, and *sinker*. Yet, while we *do* need to be prayerful and *do* need to correct wrong behaviors when identified in order to prevent depression and anxiety, guilt and shame have no helpful place in our response to illness. *Why?* Because they are irrational.

How can we blame ourselves for illness when there are genetic/familial predispositions, learned behaviors, and unrelenting crises that also contribute to the development of mind, spirit, and bodily illnesses? These factors beyond our control can cause our spirits to sink so deeply, for so long, that we may struggle to keep our heads above water, regardless of our heart for and obedience toward God.

The way in which the Holy Spirit allows us to discern the difference between illness that we can do something about and illness that requires external intervention is to listen very carefully for the truth. In the words of Rachel

Rimen, M.D., "...listening is the oldest and most powerful tool of healing...it's often the quality of our listening and not the wisdom of our words that helps others hear their own truth." I would add that listening also allows us to hear *God's wisdom* and truth since He is listening day and night—and speaks to us, as well.

> *Listening allows us to hear God's wisdom and truth.*

I've counseled a great number of depressed and anxious people. With a professional medical background of more than twenty-five years, I evaluate my client's whole being: mind, body, and spirit. Sometimes a course of medication is deemed medically necessary in order to help individuals reestablish their mind/body/Spirit balance. Yet even after some recognize there needn't be any guilt or shame over depression and anxiety, the guilt, shame, or fear of a medication intervention that has been found useful to treat their presenting symptoms can be intense.

"If I just had enough faith, I wouldn't need medicine," they tell me. "If I just believed and prayed more, I would be healed." When I hear this, I ask my client to think about all the miraculous, lifesaving interventions taking place in medical and surgical circles today. Who is to say, I ask them, that the God-given, brilliant minds of gifted medical professionals aren't a means of displaying His miraculous healing power today?

Generational, genetic, and unresolved familial dysfunctions are common elements in the development of distressing symptoms for the clients I see. Sometimes during therapy, when there seems no relief in sight from debilitating psychological symptoms, I recommend that a client see his physician in order to rule out an organic cause. If all is well on that level and the symptoms remain unrelenting, despite continued therapy and prayer, I suggest that anti-depressants or anti-anxiety medication might be considered. Some clients, however, as miserable as they may be, resist the idea strongly. Not until they understand that their physical and psychological challenges are not evidence of weakness will they accept treatment that can help alleviate their pain.

We live in an imperfect and fallen world, one that requires some to cope with illnesses that necessitate a medication intervention to get better. Does a diabetic need insulin? Most acknowledge, *yes*. But what is insulin? One of two hundred hormones in the body, it's a chemical compound that helps push sugar into the cells. Without it, we would die! Naturally, diabetics are very grateful for this medicine, which helps to regulate blood sugar and bring physical health back in balance, prevent damage to vital organs (eyes, kidneys) as well keep them alive!

Our brain also has hormones, called *neurohormones*. When these are not in balance, we might have panic attacks, depression, mania, or high anxiety, to name a few symptoms of dysfunction. Faced with such circumstances, people do find it challenging to live an emotionally stable life. Some are so devastated by the effects of imbalance they may even despair of living. The addition of psychotropic medications can help regulate the brain and bring it back into emotional and psychological balance. When that happens, health is a gift of God to them through a medication intervention.

It is essential for anyone taking psychotropic medications to understand that they are not intended to be a quick or final fix. Clients must recognize the importance of concurrent therapy to change the ways that they, unknowingly, may be contributing to the depression or anxiety and learn to practice effective coping skills. Only this combination of treatment protocols offers a potential for complete healing. In other words, we have to do *our* part. Otherwise, the misbehaving soul (our self-absorbed thoughts, emotions, and will, combined with negative self-talk), can take us off course again and lead into dangerous waters.

"I Hate Me" Messages

Persistent, emotionally induced symptoms can actually cause organic change; i.e., physical and emotional illness. A dramatic example of this occurred recently with a young woman whose language included the "I hate me" mantra. She had been telling me about the things she "hated" about her body. "I hate my stomach," she would say, for example. Although she had lost considerable weight and looked fit, the change had done nothing to resolve her self-hatred or to bring her the love and acceptance she longed for. One afternoon she shared her experience of having had a burning sensation in her stomach for some weeks and that a recent endoscopic exam had revealed a peptic ulcer. I was dismayed, but not surprised that the hatred she'd generated towards herself had hit its mark.

Compare this story with that of *Jim*—a sixty-year-old professional in the healing arts profession. He knew firsthand about the lifetime challenges brought on by chronic physical conditions. He had heart disease, painful orthopedic conditions, and respiratory disease. He normally kept a sound and positive countenance through his faith regarding his physical challenges, but he now showed up in my office with a kind of despair I had not yet before witnessed in him.

Jim had recently been diagnosed with something new: Chronic Obstructive Pulmonary Disease or COPD. Simply put, COPD is an irreversible destruction of lung cells. Although he had previously been a smoker for eleven years and had grown up in a household of secondhand smoke, amazingly he had what was considered a *mild* case. Unable to focus on that relatively positive aspect of his illness, he said to me, "Here I go again. Yet another diagnosis and more medication."

Though Jim was a mature and faithful Christian, he now found himself haunted by his old fear of and frustration with being critically ill, as feelings of helplessness came flooding back. While telling me about this, his breathing became labored. We talked and prayed about how *changing his thoughts* and words could take the wind out of his fear sails. Faith and fear blow in opposite directions, and setting our sails in the first direction will often get us moving again.

When I saw Jim a week later he actually had regained his enthusiasm for life. After time alone in prayer, Jim had remembered God's faithfulness and His promise:

All things work together for good for those who love Him and are called according to His purpose. (Romans 8:28)

Jim recognized the good in His promise right away. The *good* was another opportunity to fully trust God in all circumstances. Suddenly he understood God's *purpose* for his suffering. It was to reinforce his passion for helping others. Only through suffering himself could he authentically bring hope and healing to those around him who suffered.

God is the "God of all comfort." By trusting Him, Jim replaced the paralyzing power of his irrational fear with faith in God's power to be the prevailing wind that filled his sails.

A Sea Change

Once I discovered the power of the mind/body/Spirit connection, the focus of my day back in medical practice changed. Rather than simply listening to my patients' anatomical hearts, my passion focused on including their psychological and spiritual hearts, as well. Because of God's gracious Hand in my own physical and emotional suffering, I became a more empathetic and holistic practitioner.

I found myself questioning how my patients were feeling, aside from their physical complaints. I also found I missed opportunities for healing and patient satisfaction if I *didn't* address psychological and spiritual needs along with physical concerns. Though there is usually precious little time to address the needs of the soul in most medical practices, mine included, I would spend nearly an hour with patients, trying to discover what was going on inside them. As they spoke, I asked new questions:

- What, in the mind, was keeping them from doing better?

- What did *they* think contributed to their illness?
- What were the stressors in their lives?
- Did they understand the toll stress could take on their bodies?

I discovered that when I addressed the physical, psychological, and spiritual needs of my patients, they felt more empowered to take an active role in the process of becoming well. Once it became clear how patients simply *did better* when I spent that kind of time with them, the physicians with whom I worked began sending me their "difficult patients"—those who were not getting better despite appropriate medical interventions. I taught my patients how their minds could impact their health; my practice grew into a more holistic approach to wellness.

Astoundingly, the majority of my patients were *getting better*. I saw their lives being changed before my eyes. They felt more fulfilled, productive, and responsible for themselves. Consequently, their better choices produced better health. I could only conclude that God's healing, though always miraculous, can sometimes be seen as the natural consequence of gaining greater balance in life.

In twelve years as a physician's assistant in primary care, patient experience and medical research had shown me that over sixty percent of all doctor visits are for psychological concerns that show up as physical ailments. I decided to stop *just* practicing medicine—treating symptoms with a deeper systemic cause— and open an office as a mind/health counselor in my husband's medical clinic. I pursued further training and became a board certified *insight behavioral modification specialist*. Soon after, the Oregon Board of Medical Examiners extended my medical license to include a special designation as a clinical psychotherapist, thereby allowing clients' insurance coverage to provide for their care. I was on my way, but something was still missing. My purpose for living at that time was still self-focused. I was relying on myself and my skills, instead of relying *completely* on God.

I practiced as a mental health counselor for another eight years before I finally understood and responded to what I was meant to be: a Christ-focused therapist, a Christian counselor. My faith and God's insight to me of the mind/body/Spirit connection had proved an incredibly powerful combination. Everything from my practice to my own body had responded well to the new focus. But true *empowerment* came when I surrendered my soul to God and made my personal and professional life entirely about fulfilling His larger purposes for me.

What a change—and a *relief*—that has been! For years I struggled when my clients gave me credit for how well they did in therapy. I struggled, too, when clients blamed me when they did not do well in therapy. While I admit receiving a compliment felt a whole lot better than receiving blame, either way the shift in responsibility was not healthy for them. I knew my clients' willingness to strive for wellness by doing their soul work was *their* responsibility, not mine. My responsibility was to be the best caregiver I could be. To do that, I had to shift my clients' focus from *me* to the *True Authority*. Only then could God begin calming the stormy seas within their anxious, depressed souls.

Jesus is the Great Physician. He came to heal the sick, and for our part we are to love Him with all our soul, with our entire mind, and with all our strength. Doesn't it make sense that in disciplining ourselves to take care of our souls through worship we are also taking care of our bodies?

God is the wonderful *Master Counselor*. Now when I see clients succeed in their therapeutic journey, I know it's because they have chosen to cooperate with His authority, in agreement with right thinking and living, and have set sail on a determined course toward Sanctification. They now realize who they are in Christ and are daily discovering the treasure in the depths of their own souls.

SEVEN

---※---

Swimming Against the Tide
What You Expect, You will Realize

*"Do not conform any longer to the pattern of this world,
but be transformed by the renewing of your mind.
Then you will be able to test and approve what God's will is—
His good, pleasing, and perfect will."*

—ROMANS 12:2

When you recognize the reality of the mind/body/Spirit connection and understand how it works, you'll be motivated to move forward with your soul work. To be as healthy as possible, your will, thoughts, and emotions must function as God intended, not according to the dictates of current social fads and customs.

You may have to swim *against the tide* of the world's way of thinking—or even your own—sometimes in order to pursue your quest for Sanctification. It's challenging! In fact, you may wonder: *How can this really be done at all?*

Believe You're a Swimmer...and You Swim

If you believe either *negatively* or *positively* about an anticipated outcome in your life, chances are good you will experience what you believe to be true. If you doubt God's *desire* or *power* to heal you, your thoughts can actually prevent you from getting well. Remember, too, that although God can and will heal completely and miraculously, He may also choose *not* to heal you. In such times a trial can bring you closer to Him and provide an opportunity to build character. Choosing to maintain a positive *attitude* in suffering can build character within you and bring glory to God as you accept that He is fulfilling a greater purpose in your life.

> ...but we also rejoice in our sufferings, because we know that suffering produces perseverance; perseverance, character; and character, hope. And hope does not disappoint us, because God has poured out his love into our hearts by the Holy Spirit, whom he has given us. (Romans 5:3–5)

> *Choosing to maintain a positive attitude in suffering can build character within you and bring glory to God.*

Through the mind/body/Spirit connection your attitude can impact your path to wellness. Linda was referred to me because she had a large, deep wound on her upper left thigh that wasn't healing properly despite multiple courses of antibiotics and surgery. Her physician believed there might be underlying psychological problems contributing to her inability to heal. Linda, a trained ER nurse, was interested in approaching her medical concerns from a psychological and spiritual perspective. She was willing to investigate what might be lurking beneath her conscious mind.

During our third session Linda sat in a Lazyboy™ recliner as we began with prayer. I placed paper and crayons on a lightweight board across her lap and asked her to draw a picture of how she saw her wound. Without hesitation she quietly began. After about fifteen minutes she completed the drawing, and we prayed again. Then I asked her to talk about the picture. It showed her sitting in the chair with a blanket covering all of her except the necrotic wound on her thigh.

"Is it all right for you to tell me what this picture means?" I asked.

After a brief moment she said: "It's a picture of me sitting and healing in your Lazyboy chair. It's me feeling safe and cozy, all covered up under your blanket and getting well."

"Yes, I can see that," I said. "I'm glad you feel safe and comfortable and want your body to heal. Is there anything else that's important for me to know about your picture before we end our session today?"

"I don't think so. *Why?* Do you see anything else in the picture that's important?"

"Yes. I was wondering why the wound on your thigh isn't under the healing blanket...."

Without missing a beat, she replied: "Oh, well, that's because it's not supposed to heal."

We looked at each other in silence. I was in awe. God had just revealed a very important truth to her: *What she expected had been realized.* Her body had responded to what her mind believed.

In our next sessions an examination of Linda's past and present family circumstances helped reveal why she had perpetuated the lie that she wasn't supposed to heal. With God's grace and her own diligent soul work she gained authority over her body. The antibiotics kicked in and her next exploratory surgery revealed the core tissue of her wound had returned to normal. Both her physician husband and the surgeon were astounded by the turnabout that occurred when Linda accepted the truth that her body was *supposed to heal.*

CHOOSE *NOT* TO SINK

Negative ideas, if indulged long enough, tend to cause organic damage. *Lee,* now seventy-one and a fervent believer, has suffered with diabetes for fifty-two years. When he was sixty-two he got an influenza shot and, soon afterward, became critically ill, with unrelenting and severe pain occurring in his legs. Lee was diagnosed as having a very rare form of *vasculitis* and was placed on Prednisone and the chemotherapy drug Cytoxin. He became even sicker on the Cytoxin and was in danger of dying from the chemotherapy because of an extremely low white blood cell count. Cytoxin was replaced with another chemo drug, Imuran, and Lee remained on a regimen of this and Prednisone for several years.

Four years after this episode Lee's left eye became severely infected. He was already blind in his right eye, and this infection left him totally blind. Lee was so depressed and ill he felt like dying, a message communicated to his body. His body listened.

When Lee lost the will to be healed he got worse,

unwittingly demonstrating the power our minds have over our bodies. His doctor added a second antidepressant to help him manage suicidal thoughts and unrelenting depression, whereupon Lee became paranoid and delusional. A neurologist concluded the added antidepressant caused too much serotonin in his body. He was hospitalized, and by the time he got home didn't know how to dress or feed himself. Lee required twenty-four-hour care for three years. He looked old and very fragile. His wife thought surely she would lose him very soon.

Somewhere along the line, however, Lee made up his mind that he was going to live and experience all the blessings the Lord saw fit to give him. He chose to behave and believe he was well—and began to sing out his heartfelt love for the Lord. His health improved. Over time, his Prednisone dose was decreased to ten milligrams per day. His blood sugar levels improved enough to decrease his insulin by three units per day. His platelet count was the best ever: 288, and his cholesterol count measured 186.

Is Lee still a diabetic? Yes. Is he still blind? Yes. Does he have ongoing pain from degenerative arthritis? Yes. But Lee had made a choice that he is not going to live *under* his circumstances, but *in spite of* them. When he exercised his will in that way, his mind improved and his body responded by producing greater health.

Stay Afloat: Speak Forth Healing Words

Attitude may not be everything, but it influences your mental, physical, emotional, and spiritual health more than you know. The counselor who showed me the power of the mind/body/Spirit connection also helped me learn to replace negative thoughts with positive thoughts that reflected the truth of God's Word.

2 Corinthians 10:5 tells us to take captive every thought to the obedience of Christ. I began to reject thoughts that told me I was stupid, ugly, unlovable, and unloving, even though that's how I felt at the time. I began to speak words of health, even though I didn't feel healthy at the time. I began to create a self-portrait through words that stated the exact opposite of how I felt and what I believed about myself. In the months that followed, I must have spoken thousands of the God-filled, life-affirming words. As I did, I slowly began to get well.

When you choose to conform your thoughts to the truth of God's Word you begin to speak words that have the power to help heal your body. *Healing words* had saved my life on Sheep Mountain, when medicine was not at hand. Now they were saving and preserving my sense of self.

Feelings occur secondarily to thinking. When you think negative thoughts, you feel uncomfortable. Continuous negative thinking ultimately causes stress which, as we have seen, can depress the immune system's ability to function well and leave us vulnerable to any number of physical ailments. If you want to feel differently, you must behave differently, which begins with how you think. If you think about something good, a pleasant feeling will follow. Just as the apostle Paul said, renewing your mind can transform you both spiritually *and* physically.

At times your body suffers to such an extent that, despite your best efforts to help alleviate symptoms with healthier thinking and medicines, your body does not perceptibly respond. However, your body still benefits from exercising your mind in this way, even if it feels like you're swimming against the tide. Sometimes that's exactly what's required!

I received a phone call from a close friend recently diagnosed with Stage Four breast cancer. She said that as the news got out, a multitude of friends had poured out their hearts to her and lifted her spirits. Sometimes, however, well-meaning people send the wrong message. "Oh, Annie, it is so terrible what has happened to you," a neighbor told her. "I don't know what I would do if it happened to me, but I'm sure you will be OK. You know, my mother also had this happen to her…." Then her neighbor began to cry and blurted out, "All her hair fell out, and they took off her breasts. Oh, the *pain* she had! Not only did she suffer terribly, but the chemo gave her diabetes, which made things even worse."

When Annie finished sharing this story with me, I said to her, "Goodness, Annie, what did you do with that?"

"Well, I just ended up comforting *her,*" Annie said. "Obviously she was feeling terrible that her mother had died and she was afraid of dying herself. You know, Shelley, I have the Lord. I am not afraid of dying; though, to be honest, I *am* afraid of the suffering. But I know God will never leave me or forsake me. And that is what comforts me."

The barrage of those highly disturbing and hurtful words could have pounded Annie like unrelenting and crashing waves over her head, drowning her in fear. But she *chose* not to react that way. She swam against the tide and stayed afloat with God's comforting words, offering her compassion toward another who was suffering. Annie's most recent scan shows a positive response to cancer treatment. The tumors once embedded in her bones are gone. Yes, the right medications were given, and I also believe this healing occurred because of my friend's choice to incorporate her faith and a positive attitude into her treatment during this fearful trial in her life.

Hoisting the Proper Sail

As Annie's story demonstrates, many of us don't always respond to those who are suffering in helpful or caring ways. The tendency is to try and "fix" those who are hurting and comfort them by quoting a relevant scripture or recounting a story about our own related experience. There are times, while trying to be helpful, that we actually diminish the circumstance and feelings of the person we're trying to help with glib phrases like, "Oh, I went through this myself and I did OK," or, "Don't worry, it could be worse. I knew someone who…."

Unintentionally, by rushing in with God's Word or sharing our own or another's experience, we are creating a mechanism for *us* to feel better. That rarely helps comfort the one hurting. It is not that we don't genuinely feel for them and want them to be better, but the situation can leave us feeling helpless to do anything meaningful for those we care about. Therefore, we also suffer. Yet we have to be careful not to let our own pain or hollow comforts add to the suffering of the person we're attempting to console.

When we say things such as, "Let me know if I can do anything for you," or "Call me if you need anything," we are actually asking *them* to reach out to *us*. Most people who are hurting deeply will *not* reach out. God says: "Come to me all you who are weary and heavy laden and I will give you rest" (Matthew 11:28). And yet even the most fervent believer, when suffering, will have difficulty reaching out to God or anyone else.

So, how *can* we help? When first hearing about the

trial, begin by *affirming* them and their feelings. "I am so sorry you are going through this. Can I do anything for you right now?" "This is very sad. May I pray for you?" Follow up and pray right then if they agree. Next, call, take a meal, share a book, read from Psalms, or just sit for awhile and listen. Give your friend sufficient time for the recovery process, or his or her journey home, in their own way. This process will be different for each of us. Remember to call again after some time has passed because the support of others often wanes with time.

Liberation from unnecessary suffering while we grow for God's Glory allows us to apply our gifts and talents to the needs of others. Throughout history to the present day, thousands of books have been written proclaiming the life-enhancing effects of helping others. Most of us have experienced a sense of wellbeing when we observe and *act* to meet the needs of others. We have also experienced the relief from suffering that caring for others can bring. God's Word makes it very clear what He wants us to do:

> Offer hospitality to one another without grumbling. Each one should use whatever gift he has received to serve others, faithfully administering God's grace in its various forms. (1 Peter 4:9,10)

> Two are better than one, because they have a good reward for their labour. For if they fall, the one will lift up his fellow: but woe to him that is alone when he falleth; for he hath not another to help him up. (Ecclesiastes 4:9,10)

Whether you're trying to alleviate someone else's suffering or your own, a helpful, positive attitude will empower you to swim against the tide and align with the healing rudder of God's truth.

EIGHT

Controlling the Rudder
The Tongue Sets the Course of Your Life

*"A small rudder on a huge ship in the hands
of a skilled captain sets a course
in the face of the strongest winds.
A word out of your mouth may seem of no account,
but it can accomplish nearly anything—or destroy it!"*

—JAMES 3:4, 5 THE MESSAGE

What do you do when you hurt so deeply you can feel no gratitude in your suffering? When an *attitude adjustment* seems impossible? You need a healthy way to express your level of discomfort, yet without complaining.

> Do everything without complaining or arguing, so that you may become blameless and pure, children of God without fault. (Philippians 2:14)

When we *complain* we risk losing the support of the very people who are there to help us. Complaining sounds like blaming or whining—and it can translate to others as self-pity. Can we learn to *report* instead? Reporting sounds more like honestly sharing how we are doing, but without negative, destructive words. Report a plan of action you are choosing to help yourself feel better, and others will feel better, also!

A charming long-time friend of mine who is quite ill has had chronic pain for years and requires daily medication to relieve it. Rather than complaining that he needs *pain* pills, he reports how he is feeling with a number from one to ten, then states, "I would like my *comfort* pill now." He has noticed caregivers and family now enjoy spending time with him, and he thankfully recognizes he actually feels more comfortable, too. This has reduced his need for medication and his overall pain levels significantly.

A mindset of gratitude, regardless of the state of your health helps set you free from self-pity and increasing ill-health. Claire suffers from myriad chronic illnesses and relentless discomfort. However, she chooses her words thoughtfully in order to increase wellness. She refuses to say things like, "Why do I have to be going through this? What have I done wrong to deserve this?" or simply, "Why me?" She is thoughtful before responding to otherwise well-meaning comments like, "Are you hanging in there OK?"

Considering the picture that phrase brings to mind, she chooses to answer, "I am not willing to just hang in there. I choose instead to stand on God's promises and thrive."

> I can do all things through Christ who gives me strength. (Philippians 4:13)

> I will never leave thee, nor forsake thee. (Hebrews 13:5, KJV)

In describing our circumstances through reporting rather than complaining, our body has the opportunity to respond in a more constructive way, one that can provide greater comfort. This, in turn, allows our body to reach its fullest potential for health.

THE RUDDER SETS THE COURSE

How you choose to communicate is a critical part of the soul factor. *Why?* Brain chemicals that either *enhance* or *thwart* your body are released with every thought throughout every day of your life. When you express thoughts with negative words that speak against others or yourself, you are communicating in a way that will crush your spirit and potentially hasten the death of the body. What you speak can be either a *blessing* or a *curse*. So, we are literally speaking blessings or curses to others and to ourselves every time we open our mouths.

"Sticks and stones can break my bones, but names (words) can never harm me," is an old saying I used frequently in childhood. Because raw sores from eczema covered most of my skin as a young person, some people would call me names, like "ugly weirdo girl," or "the leper kid." When they did, I couldn't help but repeat those words over and over in my mind. Unfortunately, the old adage is wrong. Names *are* like sticks and stones, they *do* hurt, and they cause serious emotional problems when they're received deeply in your spirit, becoming a self-fulfilling prophecy.

Some years ago I received a call from an old friend, Emma. She had just been released from a hospital back East. In severe emotional crisis she had attempted to commit suicide, which for her was a cry for help. She received immediate intervention, but would need ongoing therapy to complete her recovery process. At the lowest point in her fifty years of life, she asked if she could fly out and spend some time with me.

During Emma's stay we both prayed that God would be the Master Counselor when we gathered together in His Name. Indeed, He *was* present and led us both to one of her core beliefs—the word *ugly*. Although a beautiful woman now, during childhood other kids had called her ugly because she had red hair, freckles, and protruding ears. By the end of her visit, the Lord had revealed to her that she wasn't ugly, but rather, *different*. This is not simply psychological double talk. She was liberated from her destructive thinking. She'd learned from studying God's Word that He's created everyone uniquely different. Emma wasn't ugly; she was *unique!*

In order to fully embrace this new concept, my friend began her "shower work," allowing healing warm water to flow over her body while the word *unique* flowed through her mind, washing away the word *ugly*. There was more to discover and correct regarding her thinking, but that one word—*unique*—was the key to helping set her free from a belief that had undermined her entire life: *I'm ugly*.

When we examine the power of words we begin to understand their connection to feelings. Mention the name of a loved one and positive images that evoke powerful feelings automatically appear. Conversely, naming an illness often conjures up images with strong negative feelings attached. If the thoughts are left unchallenged, those negative emotions can lead to psychological or physical illness. In effect, the words we use to talk about a disease, illness, or injury can lead us to think that (rather than experiencing the symptoms of an illness) we *are* the illness.

Sometimes the medical community unintentionally reinforces this notion. On my first job after medical school I overheard a doctor refer to a patient as *"the bipolar* down the hall."

When staff was overloaded with patients and running behind, it wasn't unusual to hear someone say, "What room is *the bleeding ulcer* in?" or, "Is *the strep throat* still waiting in room five?" Until I came to realize how powerfully words could affect health and wellbeing, I was often guilty of this myself!

The truth is that words that define you by your illness will diminish your capacity to heal. Sometimes you may use the name of a current illness to describe yourself out of habit, or because you don't know better. Certainly, there are people, who *do* define themselves in this way in hopes of garnering sympathy from others. Admittedly, I did this very thing for years. Yet it only perpetuated an unhealthy behavior, impacting both my psychological and physical healing. Remember, the soul and body are connected! So, it is helpful to *refuse to take ownership* of an illness by saying, for example, *my* cancer. Rather, refer to *the* cancer as something that may be there, but is not part of *you*.

THE RUDDER IS SMALL, BUT MIGHTY

Just as we don't have to accept the destructive words we hear, we don't have to speak destructive words, either. The little word *but*, for example, can be very powerful. The moment someone says *but*, we inevitably hear *only* what follows it. Think about it.

- "I love you, but…."
- "I want to be with you, but…."
- "I want to be well, but…."

In each case the word *but* negates the preceding phrase. Typically, when someone uses the word, we don't even remember how the sentence started. We hear only the last part:

- "…I need to talk about some things."
- "…I just don't have the time."
- "…it costs too much to see a doctor."

The word *but* turns a positive thought into a negative statement. What we hear is:

- "…I don't like you."
- "…you're not worth my time."
- "….I'm not worth the money it takes to see the doctor."

By changing just *one word,* we can send a different message:

- "I love you, *and* I would like to talk about some things."

- "I want to be with you, *and* since my time is short now, let's get together tonight."
- "I want to be well, *and* I have some financial challenges I want to work out."

Another small but powerful little word is *try*. Depending on the context, by using this word we can be telling others and ourselves that we are *not* going to do something. When I think of the word try, it says to me, "Maybe I will, and maybe I won't." So, which is it? I hear clients say they'll *try* to do their homework or will *try* to pay attention to their language or will *try* to apologize to a loved one. It's clear they aren't actually yet ready to *do it* at all.

Sometimes one word can make all the difference in getting a positive rather than a negative response from another. When we preface a statement with *"why,"* some jump to the conclusion that the questioner is saying something negative or critical about them. Suppose your well-meaning spouse asks you, "Why did you leave the lights on in the garage?" Your subconscious can easily interpret the question as a personal attack, triggering you to feel defensive.

While the word *why* asks a question about the person, the word *what* asks a question about the circumstance. "The lights in the garage were on all night. What happened?" This question allows the person to whom it's addressed to say what happened without provoking a defensive response. "Oh, I went to get some ice cream out of the freezer last night and forgot to turn off the lights. I'm sorry about that." Amazingly, changing your language in small ways can steer the conversation toward a positive or negative conclusion; i.e., the tongue sets the course in human interactions.

> ...take ships as an example. Although they are so large and are driven by strong winds, they are steered by a very small rudder, wherever the pilot wants to go. (James 3:4–6)

We have the power to use our rudder (tongue) to steer us in the right direction, toward healthier word choices. This power resides in our soul, and exercising it is part of the soul work that promotes healing and Sanctification. Even if you don't *feel* like doing it, you can *will* yourself to think and speak in a less provoking, healing manner.

THE PILOT TAKES THE WHEEL

A wheel is connected to a ship's rudder. You are the pilot of your ship, and your soul is the wheel that controls the rudder, which is your tongue. To stay on course, each of us must learn to *speak the truth in love* to ourselves, as well as to others.

> *To stay on course, all of us must learn to speak the truth in love to ourselves, as well as to others.*

These skills rarely come naturally or easily, particularly if early childhood experiences have taught us to perceive ourselves as unlovable. As did I, most of my clients need to learn to communicate their feelings, needs, and concerns to themselves and others in a way that does not bring harm. Let's look at one man who did so.

Albert started therapy believing he was unlovable. His fifth wife had just divorced him, and he wanted to learn why he kept ending up with "bad spouses." He was beginning to suspect that perhaps something about him might be contributing to the unhappiness experienced in all of his marriages, and he was becoming open to change.

During therapy one of the insights gained was that Albert chose women who fell "in love" with him quickly—and he with them. They would agree to marry after only a few weeks or months of dating. Inside, both mates felt unlovable and, since they didn't know themselves or know how to communicate effectively, the relationship was on a collision course with disaster right from the beginning.

In one session Albert exclaimed, "I hate being alone!" He added that when he was with someone else, no matter *who* it was, he felt more secure and less uneasy about life in general. "Why am I this way?" he asked me. "I'm so tired of making the wrong choices. I don't want this anymore! Why do I keep doing this?"

"Do you really want to know?" I asked him. "The answer may be painful to hear."

Albert nodded, *yes*.

I asked him to place his hands in front of him, palms up and imagine himself placing the words "*I hate*" in his left palm, and the words "*being alone*" in his right palm. When he'd done this, I asked him to read the words he'd placed in his left palm. Tentatively, he said, "I hate?"

"Yes," I said, "Now read the words you've placed in your right palm."

"Being alone?"

"Yes. Now tell me, *who* is alone?"

"*Me?*"

"Correct. Now, replace "*being alone*" with "*me*" in your right palm."

Hesitantly, he responded, "OK."

"Now read the words in your palms from left to right."

Albert stopped speaking. Tears ran down his face as he read aloud, "I hate…*me.*"

The tongue is mighty. It will steer us in whatever direction *we* choose. Without *controlling* it or *paying attention* to where it is taking us, however, we are apt to sail straight into the deadly trap of either one or the other sea monster, *Charybdis* or *Scylla*. Instead, set your rudder faithfully to keep your ship on course toward Sanctification. Realign it daily by the Morning Star of God's truth.

NINE

Steering by a True Compass
It May Be *our* truth, but Is it *the* Truth

*"The word of God is living and active,
sharper than any double-edged sword,
it penetrates even to dividing soul and spirit, joints and marrow;
it judges the thoughts and attitudes of the heart."*

—HEBREWS 4:12

God's compass, *The Holy Bible,* is a collection of sixty-six books full of poetry, wisdom, personal example, life stories, and metaphors that illustrate universal truths. As a health care professional, a Christian, and a person with a lengthy history of illness, I find it imperative to incorporate biblical truth into an all-encompassing model of good health. As I work with those who come to me, I must be careful my therapeutic techniques are always congruent with

Scripture. Clients must be *active* participants rather than *passive* recipients of God's Word. I encourage them to discover the path God intends—and to make an *active* choice to pursue it.

As we begin therapy, clients seek to identify the roots of their emotional or physical illness through standard therapeutic processes and by exploring God's Word. I make every effort to remain open to what the client is bringing, without expectations about how they're *supposed* to change in order to "be better," or "get more Christ-like." Throughout my time with a client, I remain detached from the outcome of his or her choices, since guiding them directly is the work of the Holy Spirit. My role is simply to point out the compass.

God's Charted Course

The mind cannot hold two opposing ideas as truth at the same time. Trying to do so causes us deep conflict that will ultimately take its toll on our mind, body, and spirit. This is especially true when we're confronted with *right* or *wrong* behavior. Unless we resolve it in a way that leaves us right with God, intense moral conflict can lead to certain despair. In Romans 2, Scripture tells us when we know we are doing wrong, God holds us accountable. *Knowing* His Word *but not following* it makes all the difference with God, and our God-given conscience rebukes us.

When clients come to see me and say, "I'm just so *confused*. I don't know what to do," it is frequently a case of intense *moral conflict,* rather than confusion. One case in point was when *Edie* shared she was having difficulty getting along with her second husband, whom she described as being "too controlling." She had recently seen her physically abusive first husband at church and thought he seemed *changed* since he was very kind to her there. She felt guilty and wondered if she had been wrong in divorcing him in the first place. Now she fantasized about getting back together with him. She said she was *confused* because she knew her thoughts were out of alignment with God's Word and because she didn't want to hurt her current husband, yet her thoughts were very powerful.

I suggested to Edie that her underlying faith and deep desire to live rightly was probably causing her moral conflict, not *confusion*. She was attempting to hold onto an idea that was in opposition to her beliefs as a Christian woman. Once she understood she was *conflicted* and not confused, Edie began to get back into the Word. When she did, she realized the right thing to do was to stay married, own up to the consequences of her past decision, recognize she was forgiven, and move forward.

Cleansing Daily in the Word—with SOAP

God designed our bodies to respond to our soul and spirit. Therefore, we must *train* our body to take action upon the Word of God, conforming our behavior to its counsel. When we do this, our behavior will become congruent with God's desire for our lives. Of course, it doesn't hurt to have a good reminder and a practical tool at hand during the training process!

In medical school we learned to take a complete medical and social history of a patient. We were taught the acronym SOAP (Subjective, Objective, Assessment, and Plan) as a way to remember what we needed to include in our presentation of a case to our preceptor physician, who would then determine if our conclusions were correct.

SOAP was a method that served my patients' needs well. It provided a systematic way for me to understand what patients required *from me* and helped patients recognize what they needed to do *for themselves*. Providing a clear plan of action, the effectiveness of this method continues to be relevant in my therapy practice today.

Years later, much to my delight, I found that my church was also using SOAP as an acronym device. The purpose was to assist Christians to read the Bible daily in a way that would help them grow spiritually. Washing daily with SOAP requires discipline but, like *any* change for the better, once it becomes a habit the rewards can be tangible. Life can improve.

In the SOAP method, we create a daily opportunity to write out what God's Spirit seems to be speaking to us individually. It goes like this:

S—Scripture: Identify the Scriptures that speak to you in your daily reading.

O—Observation: Figure out what message God is giving to His actual readers (usually the plain and obvious meaning).

A—Application: How does this observation apply to you personally? What does God want you to know, be, do, etc., because of it…?

P—Prayer: Ask God's assistance to implement your personal application through a brief written prayer.

Using the SOAP approach to daily Bible study will add to your deepening conviction about the course God has set for you and help you self-correct on your quest toward Sanctification. The mind/body/Spirit connection shows how your thoughts affect every cell of your body. Studying

Scripture and acting on what it says ensures that you will have the mind of Christ. As you make certain your thoughts reflect the mind of Christ, your "soul work" assists in this process, enhancing the body's natural, spontaneous healing.

Nevertheless, until you *act* on the truth of what God says to you through Scripture, He cannot guide you, soothe you, teach you, or make you more like Jesus. When you do act on His truth, He will heal your soul through the demonstration of your faith. And with that spiritual healing, your *physical* body also gains its highest potential for healing. Cleansing yourself daily with God's SOAP will slough off the grime and reset your compass point in the direction of God's perfect will for your life's journey.

Ten

Sailing Upright
Proper Maintenance Makes for a Seaworthy Ship

"In this you greatly rejoice, though now for a little
while you may have had to suffer grief in all kinds of trials.
These have come so that your faith—of greater worth than gold,
which perishes even though refined by fire—
may be proved genuine and may result in praise, glory,
and honor when Jesus Christ is revealed."

1 PETER 1:6, 7

To sail in an upright position on water, a ship must maintain balance. If it tips or heels too far to the right or left in high winds it can capsize. Even so, your mind, body, and spirit must be like a well-balanced ship. If all *three* are not in proper balance, the slightest spiritual wind can tip you over. At times you may be unsteady, yet earnestly doing God's work. Remember, it is all about the *process of balancing*, not that you will always be in *perfect* balance.

Oswald Chambers writes in *My Utmost for His Highest*:

"God does not want to make us perfect, but rather His purpose is to make us one with Him." Likewise, making the *effort* to balance your life helps keep you upright as you sail toward your goal of optimal health and Sanctification.

In fact, health is much more than the absence of sickness. It is the conscious pursuit of the highest spiritual, mental, emotional, physical, environmental, and social aspects of the human experience. Seeking balance in these things is the special work of the soul.

OFF KILTER

My experiences, and those of my clients, have shown me clearly that every thought causes a physical reaction. And it works the other way, as well. A serious physical disease can cause a negative state of mind. Let me share a bit from my personal life history.

In 1999 my private practice was doing well, my personal life was satisfying, and my marriage was strong. In short, I was enjoying every minute! Then things began to change. I tired more easily, had bouts of pneumonia, and began to feel depressed. I found myself being overly sensitive, distraught, and discouraged. What I didn't know was that my mood and energy levels were changing because a cancer had been growing and spreading into my thyroid and lymph system for at least five years. The physical changes had been slow and subtle, so I'd attributed the bothersome symptoms to the aging process. I was wrong.

Is it any wonder my emotions were so out of kilter? My body and soul were out of balance. And because I had not yet cooperated with God's ultimate plan for me, my spirit was also out of balance. My ship was being swamped, and I was lilting fast!

Surgical intervention and subsequent nuclear-medicine treatments proved a total success. Once the physical problem was taken care of and correct medications assigned, my emotions stabilized and my energy and zest for life again returned. Structurally, my ship was being repaired, but it would be some years still before it was fully upright and ready to move full speed ahead.

'SHIPMATES'

In pursuit of a balanced vessel, a health care provider and his patient are not like captain and deckhand; they are *shipmates,* with different duties. Pursuing a holistic self-care approach to health means you'll examine the underlying causes of an illness with your physician or counselor. Next, you'll explore options for effective treatment together. The holistic approach of an alert physician will not ignore the role of the psychological responses on the body to current physical experience. Neither will an aware counselor neglect the role of physiological events on the mind. When we are unwell in any way we must remind ourselves—*and our health care providers*—to view the illness as a manifestation of the whole person, not just as an isolated event.

Ideally the healthcare provider/patient relationship will consider the needs, desires, awareness, and insights of the patient, as well as those of the practitioner. After suitable treatment options are identified, it is preferable for patients to make choices in their care. Yes, we professionals can make suggestions and offer as thorough an evaluation as possible, but in the end patients fare better if they choose their course of treatment and follow through on their own accord.

My experience as a Christian therapist tells me that without God's Word and personal faith combining, the healing process is incomplete—like towing a sinking ship into dry dock, but not performing *all* the needed repairs. An optimum state of health depends on employing all resources at our disposal so we are as seaworthy as possible.

> *When we are unwell in any way, we must remind ourselves—and our health care providers— to view the illness as a manifestation of the whole person and not just as an isolated event.*

Once we factor in personal faith, the quality of the relationship between the patient and practitioner becomes a major determinant of healing outcomes. Practitioners must remember that the personal example we set in living out habits that make for wellness will give rise to our patients' greater expectations of healing. If we don't live as we recommend, we can undermine a patient's belief in the healing process.

The realization that God has pre-programmed profound healing powers within us helps enable our bodies to heal as we do our part and trust that this process is in motion. When you break a bone, for example, practitioners will immobilize the break, but it is the body that knits the bone together. In calling forth our innate healing capabilities, we look to God's mechanisms within for healing, as much as we look to external sources of a cure.

Healed or Cured on the Voyage?

Though most of us may assume that *healing* and *curing* mean the same thing, understanding the subtle difference helps guide us along the pathway to good health. *Healing* generally refers to what happens *within* a patient's body, mind, or spirit that resolves a physical, psychological, or spiritual problem. Healing involves the *whole* person. *Curing*, however, usually refers to what a health care provider does to/for the patient's body.

After a surgical or medical intervention has cured my patient I will say, "Now, it's time to enter into the healing process." Some people understand, but others will say, "What do you mean? I'm *cured* now. I don't have that problem anymore."

I answer this way. "You are right. Your body no longer has this problem; however, your mind has not fully accepted that. So, now you might consider choosing thoughts and words that eliminate any irrational fear that may remain, thus enhancing and completing your healing process."

Curing may remove the symptoms of a disease through outside influences and interventions, but it usually leaves the underlying *cause* of the symptoms untouched. In this sense, curing may have only a temporary, comforting effect on the disease. Healing, on the other hand, is about effective therapy, no matter how it comes about, that supports God's healing, along with the body's natural response to it.

I know God can heal. In 1994, He healed me miraculously of eosinophilic gastroenteritis (EG), which had plagued me since childhood. In 1994 I had been on large amounts of Prednisone for several months to relieve the debilitating effects of EG. Along with several other medications that brought me some relief, the nature of these medications could dramatically shorten my lifespan. After traveling to interview Dr. Larry Dossey on his new book, *Healing Words: The Power of Prayer in Medicine,* for my community television series on alternative medicine, I decided, for the first time in my life, to pray for healing during the flight home. I received a healing—and later was able to stop the harsh medications. (Please talk to your doctor before *you* consider stopping any medications; each person's experience may be unique and different.)

We know that miracles can and *do* happen. During the last several years, despite the toll of cancer and other physical challenges, I've enjoyed the best physical, emotional, and spiritual health of my entire life. Although I'm not completely cured, through my healing process I am no longer challenged by constant or debilitating symptoms and pain, and I consider myself well into the process of being fully healed. I know the medications I line up and consume each day are lifesaving, critical components in this healing, as are my thoughts and words about my own health.

The fact that I am *healed spiritually* has been the most important part of my healing process. When I finally grasped the difference this made in my physical and psychological health, I chose to submit myself to God. Many people have been cured and healed by God. Although God may not choose to give everyone a complete, immediate physical cure, if we ask to be healed spiritually, He will see to it through the truth of His Word.

My greatest concern for clients is for those who are ill and who may not really *want* to be well. *How can this be true?* Becoming well may mean a loss of identity, which provides for *attention* or a *sense of control*. Some may rely emotionally on others' concern for them. Ironically, *not getting well* can be a way of manipulating others to stay in the relationship. Others fear experiencing what they imagine to be a new and difficult identity. I know *just* how they feel. That's how it once was for me.

Maybe *you* don't want to submit to God's will and practice the disciplines necessary for maintaining your health. Why, or why not? Some factors are in your power. Remember, Jesus asked the beggar who sought healing from Him, "Do you want to be healed?"

It's not that some won't be challenged by illness and injury throughout life, but you don't have to be *soul-sick* in the process. You can either be controlled by your illness or you can choose to *control your attitude* when responding to an illness's impact on you. The amount of energy either takes is essentially the same.

Preventative Maintenance

God is pleased when we maintain our earthly vessel, His special creation and gift to each one of us. With proper maintenance, you can often avoid illness and its challenging treatment protocol, which is preferable, yet requires a patient to play a larger role in her own preventative care. When illness *does* come upon us, lifestyle modifications stand out over drugs and surgery as initial therapeutic options.

Some of my clients, concerned about being too self-focused and selfish, wonder if they are being dysfunctional in their approach to self care. Nothing could be further from the truth! In fact, I gently remind them, *not* taking care of yourself is actually selfish. *Selfishness* is when we see dry rot in our hull and do little or nothing to repair it, then keep sailing the high seas, expecting the Coast Guard to come to our rescue when our boat springs a leak. The healthier, more responsible approach is to do whatever is required to service and maintain a sound ship.

Some hesitate to engage in proper self care because they see it as too much work. Indeed, most humans are likely to take *the path of least resistance* and do what is easiest—or do nothing at all. I can relate to that style, having exhibited it myself for quite a while. But, sailors beware! Over time, the path of least resistance will actually take you down *the path of least existence*! One of the fruits of the Spirit in Galatians, Chapter Five, is self-control. And although that gift's potential lies deep within us, you have to exercise it—*like a muscle*—in order for self-control to become strong and aid in prevention.

It helps to remember our greatest role model: Jesus

Christ. When Jesus was joyful, He laughed; when hungry, He ate; when worried, He prayed; when depressed, He wept; when tired, He slept, and when angry, He took corrective action, as in the temple at Jerusalem with the money changers. He also removed Himself from potentially harmful situations in order to preserve Himself for the moment of His ultimate calling at Calvary. In other words, Jesus took care of Himself in ways that kept His Body, Mind, and Spirit in balance so He could fulfill God's highest calling on His life.

THE NEGATIVE EFFECTS OF STRESS

Stress, or the pressure to change and act beyond what feels familiar or comfortable, is a part of life. In some ways, much of your circumstances lie beyond your control, and stress is inevitable. *Change happens.* And, whether you perceive a change as a positive or a negative event, it can unleash an adrenalin response that takes a negative toll on your body.

While you can't always control the stressors in your life, you can help your body recover from stress's inevitable effects by deliberately making time to recover. Building a new house or starting a new job can be energizing, but even this kind of excitement will initiate a tremendous experience of stress and fatigue.

When you refuse to take the time needed for stress recovery because you want to accomplish something of importance to you or another, you just may relinquish the ability to accomplish *anything* of importance to God. Letting stress mount unchecked, or responding to stress in an unhealthy manner, throws you off balance and accelerates death.

Stress can overwhelm you at times, capsizing your plans. I know—it has *me*. On occasion, you might even imagine that being someone else would be better or easier than being who you are. I sometimes ask my patients to imagine exchanging another person's life problems for their own. *No takers so far.* It usually boils down to the fact that if you must suffer, you'll usually choose to carry your own stuff rather than take on another person's suffering. It makes sense because God gives you grace to bear your own, not another's suffering. He created you with a unique ability to handle whatever He allows in your life.

> No temptation has seized you except what is common to man. And God is faithful; he will not let you be tempted beyond what you can bear. But when you are tempted, he will also provide a way out so that you can stand up under it. (1 Corinthians 10:13)

Again, we can't change the nature of our being, but we can change the nature of our soul when we ask Christ to be our strength in all things.

> *Letting stress mount unchecked, or responding to stress in an unhealthy manner, throws you off balance and accelerates death.*

God created you uniquely for His own purposes. In Job 36:15 says: "Those who suffer He delivers in their suffering; He speaks to them in their affliction." Note that He delivers you "in" and not "from" your troubles. That means you *will* suffer at times in your life. Yet so much of your suffering comes from misplaced desires or from wanting something other than what you have.

Frequently, we are not willing to wait on God for relief from stress, or for blessing. We want *what* we want, *when* we want it, and that means *right now.* It's not that instant gratification is necessarily bad, or that nothing good can come from it. But if we are not willing to defer gratification and wait on God, we may miss out on something much better than the "good" thing we think we want: we may forfeit His very "best" for us.

We also suffer when we fail to forgive the real or imagined, intentional or unintentional, hurts others have inflicted upon us. God frees us from guilt and stress when we seek and accept His forgiveness for the wrongs we've committed against others. We free ourselves when we forgive others for the way they've wronged us…and forgive ourselves, also.

ELEVEN

Storms and Treacherous Shoals
The Fullness of God's Love Is Revealed in Suffering

We will no longer be infants, tossed back and forth by the waves,
and blown here and there by every wind...

—EPHESIANS 4:14

To step into the life God has for us we must change our way of thinking. If we hold on to thought patterns left over from disappointing, wounding experiences, or from rejecting God's forgiveness, these negative perceptions, *lies*, can become our truth, making it difficult to hear God's Voice express His present intentions for our lives.

PURPOSEFUL, OR *POINTLESS* SUFFERING?

Jennifer, at middle-age, had held a lie in her subconscious for decades. After her tearful confession of two teen pregnancy terminations, she said she believed God had forgiven her. When asked if she had been able to forgive *herself,* she answered in the affirmative.

Wondering why she continued to sob, I asked, "So, you feel *full* forgiveness from Him and for yourself?"

Speaking with conviction she said, "Yes, I do… particularly since what I did is such an *unforgivable* sin."

Tragically, it was clear that Jennifer had *not* received God's forgiveness, nor had forgiven herself, for the sins of her youth. She was continually tossed and buffeted by waves of guilt. I shared with her the truth that *yes,* sin can be forgiven!

> If we confess our sins, he is faithful and just and will forgive us our sins and purify us from all unrighteousness. (1 John 1:9)

That day she made a recommitment to Christ and truly received the fullness of His forgiveness and love.

God doesn't take pleasure in human suffering, nor does He want us to suffer. He *allows* suffering because He has things to teach us that we may only be able to learn through affliction. He allows what is necessary to fashion us into a well-built, well-maintained ship so we can safely ride out the swells of any storm. The Bible is very clear that not only does God *allow* suffering, but that we should *expect* it in our lives at times as part of the human experience, which Jesus endured and modeled to us:

> In bringing many sons to glory, it was fitting that God, for whom and through whom everything exists, should make the author of their Salvation [Jesus] perfect through suffering. (Hebrews 2:10)

If we are to be like Christ we will suffer, as He did. My goal in therapy is to help clients discern whether God is molding and refining them through painful experiences or they are engaging in self-inflicted suffering. Once they discern what is happening, they can work with their suffering in a proactive manner.

SEAWORTHINESS

For people of faith it isn't usually the fear of dying that challenges us the most. There are days when we who experience the effects of chronic conditions, physical or psychological, can wish that the suffering was just *over*. It is not that we want to die, but we *would* like to skip over the process of getting there, however long that takes! What challenges us most is continuing to suffer, whether through pain, fatigue, anxiety, or depression. *How can we expect to accomplish anything for God when we haven't received total or obvious healing,* we wonder? *How can God use us to help others while we continue to know suffering?*

We put suffering in proper perspective when we learn to accept *what is,* as well as *what can be* learned by obediently surrendering to God's will in our lives daily. It may be His will that we endure suffering. When we *are* suffering, our choice is clear. We can grumble, or we can be humbled. When experiencing prolonged or serious pain and illness, most of us start grumbling. This does not mean we shouldn't seek to reduce pain and suffering when it is available to us through medical, psychological, or spiritual help.

But just think how differently you feel when you're not grumbling! When you choose to speak or even smile with a constructive attitude, even if you don't feel like doing it, your body responds in a healthier way. It is then God will give you a greater ability to understand yourself and His purpose for your life. You will begin to empathize with others' vulnerability and pains, helping them realize both their potential and God's purpose for their lives.

It reminds me of *Charles,* a recovering alcoholic who came to see me with an advancing and painful chronic rheumatoid arthritis. He felt hopeless, angry, of no value to anyone. The thought of having to take medication daily really bothered him. I shared my own ongoing challenges and God-focused way of thinking with him, and for the first time he began to feel affirmed and understood. He embraced His faith and love of the Lord in a new way. Today he leads an inspiring ministry, where he walks alongside and lifts up those who also endure this kind of suffering.

We cannot offer other people hope and healing until we ourselves have come through the *refining* process. This is not dependent on whether or not we have found complete physical or psychological healing, and it can't be offered in our own strength, either. When we try to do so, the best we can offer is "fools gold." I know, for that was all I had to offer when I first started my medical/counseling practice. I talked a good and honest talk. I mistakenly believed, however, that I had to be *completely* physically cured before I could consider myself truly healed. Until I saw success from *God's* perspective—that healing is a process—and understood His refining process, I wasn't as effective in touching the lives of the deeply wounded and hopeless. At least, not in the way I now can be.

The Bible is quite clear: God gave His only Son so that our sins could be forgiven. Though we live in a world, full of much potential suffering, God will see to it that our suffering is not meaningless. Indeed, it is full of His purpose, contributing to the accomplishment of His excellent plan for us.

Christ suffered through the Crucifixion in order to pay for all the wrongs and transgressions we commit in life. He also suffered, "for the joy that was set before him," says Hebrews 12:2. Just as Christ's suffering was necessary to accomplish our Salvation and His joy, our own suffering may be necessary for our full Sanctification and ultimate joy. Suffering can be a refinement, and disease or injury is often part of that process.

PERILOUS SEAS

With the help of the mind/body/Spirit connection, we *can* remain seaworthy even while riding the most perilous swells of a raging sea. Let's look at someone who did.

A few years back *Myra* came to see me. She had accepted Christ as her Lord and Savior, but had yet to choose to surrender her life to Him. Her patterns of behavior were proving more and more destructive, and her relatives had finally encouraged her to get help.

In her early forties, Myra's challenges included alcohol abuse, drug use, and a pattern of choosing abusive relationships. By the age of eighteen she had been married, had given birth to a child, and had been divorced. She had never had a steady or safe relationship with a man. One of the reasons she'd agreed to get help now was that her live-in boyfriend had assaulted her and her thirteen year-old daughter. Even though she hadn't been willing to save herself, deep down Myra knew she had to save her daughter.

Our first meeting was heart-wrenching. Myra had been

abused for so long it would be weeks before she would be able to see violence for what it was. She believed she really loved the man who was beating her and that he felt the same towards her, as well. We discussed at length what *real love* between healthy people looked like and how a relationship in which someone physically and verbally abused her and her daughter did not really fit that picture.

"I still can't give him up, because I love him," she said. "He really is a good man underneath. He apologizes sometimes. When we first met, he was funny and wonderful to be with. He made me feel so good inside."

"Could it be that what you love is what you *wanted* him to be, or *hoped* he would be, rather than what he has *revealed* himself to be?" I asked.

Myra remained silent for several moments. Forlorn, she looked up and began to cry.

"I know God loves me and has forgiven me, but I just don't know how to do things differently," she said. "I don't know how to find a better life for myself, so I just keep waiting for God to do something."

I prayed silently for a moment, and then said, "You know, Myra, Scripture says in Mark 8 that those who try to find their life shall lose it, but those who lose their life for His sake shall find it. Are you ready to lose your life, such as it is, and find the life God has waiting in store for you?"

Myra was ready to escape the dangers of the perilous sea waves she sailed. In time she learned the importance of submitting to a proper and loving authority, rather than an unloving, abusive one. After two years of persevering in prayer, Bible study, and doing her soul work in therapy, she is now clean, sober, and in a new relationship with a kind, Christian man who shares her obedience to and love for God.

Smooth Sailing

It is often scary and painful for people to examine the labyrinth of rationalizations and denials that perpetuate their suffering. While doing this, clients usually cry. Their tears are quite therapeutic, since crying produces a chemical response that helps us feel better. The relief isn't just emotional, either, since the human brain has receptors that produce opiates. Opiate receptors receive these opiates, then release chemicals called *endorphins* that create in us a pleasant emotional state. When we cry, endorphins begin to flow through our entire body and enhance our immune system.

There are other ways to trigger the immune system to respond positively, however. Throughout the centuries, for instance, people have known and utilized the power of healing derived from touching and caring for animals.

Maggie, my first therapy cat, who joined me as I worked with clients, taught me firsthand that contact with an animal can bring significant relief to otherwise unremitting physical and emotional pain. When she died at age twenty I felt deeply the loss of her many contributions to my wellbeing, and I cried for several days.

After a time of mourning, Ken and I went to the Humane Society. There we found a six-month-old, flame-tipped Siamese kitten we named *Barnabas,* whose biblical name means "the encourager."

When we got Barnabas home we started the training process to prepare him for the constant flow of people coming into my home office. His name has proven prophetic. Many times, in special moments with my feline-friendly clients, Barnabas makes his appearance as if on cue. He meows his hello at my door as if to ask, "May I come in?" When invited, he steps in and meows, "How are you?" Without further ado, he takes a seat up on the couch, leaning against the client or curling up directly in his or her lap. The peace that comes over both feline and client is a sight to behold. My own heart is always softened and relieved, also. The more someone strokes Barnabas, the better they both feel.

Animal contact is just one example of the important role our five senses play in enhancing our body's immune system and our overall sense of wellbeing. Stimulating our senses in pleasurable ways—through laughing, eating, exercising, worshipping, reading, or listening to beautiful music, to name a few such activities—releases endorphins into the bloodstream. The effect is to diminish pain and reduce stress, enhancing our immune system's ability to heal the body.

Principles of the mind/body/Spirit connection tell us that the opposite also holds true. When we reflect on past or present negative experiences, or look fearfully toward the future, we don't feel well. It can be helpful to visit those thoughts and emotions so we can learn from them, and hopefully steer away from the undercurrent of self-inflicted suffering, but dwelling on—or *in*—the negative for too long is unhealthy overall.

Staying in unsafe relationships and having little understanding of appropriate boundaries, for example, is like diving headlong into shark-infested waters. In Drs. Townsend and Cloud's landmark book, *Boundaries*, a healthy boundary is compared to human skin. Its function is to keep the *good in* and the *bad out*. If we have early life wounds that have left us "bleeding" emotionally, we must take active responsibility to get ourselves healed in order to avoid further, unnecessary, or self-destructive suffering. When in an unhealthy or hurtful relationship, then, it's good to remember: if you are already bleeding, don't swim with sharks!

> *If you are bleeding emotionally,
> don't swim with sharks!*

In contrast, a long-time friend who lives the mind/body/Spirit connection offers an example of constructive, sanctified suffering. Over the years she has had to cope with the challenges that come with having a disabled son. In a luncheon conversation, this faithful woman of God quoted the Scripture that has held her steadfast for years:

> Then they cried to the LORD in their trouble, and
> he saved them from their distress. (Psalm 107:13)

My friend said she realized God used her years of sacrifice to provide her disabled son with the education and training necessary for his independence. She states she could not have done this on her own. She also knows God brought her through those difficult years to demonstrate His faithfulness to *her*. With the infirmities of her aging years encroaching, she now sees that God used her dedication to her son to provide for her, also. Indeed, had God not helped her take care of him in his younger years, her son would not be there to care for her now. Surprising ports of destination: they're just one way God uses our suffering to reveal His grace-filled intention for our lives.

Twelve

At the Helm
Who's in Control?

"May God Himself, the God of peace,
Sanctify you through and through.
May your spirit, soul, and body be kept blameless
at the coming of our Lord Jesus Christ.
The One who calls you is faithful, and He will do it."

— 1 Thessalonians 5:23, 24

It took me awhile to follow the course God set for my life, in part because I thought I had to be at the helm of my own ship, hands firmly gripping the wheel. I assumed if I aimed for godly goals, He would reward me with immediate success. But I had to learn that God's desires aren't about our accomplishments. He wants us to use the special talents and gifts He has given us, but He is much more interested in what we are *becoming* than in what we are *achieving*. To become what God intends us to be, He must be at the helm of our vessel.

Response vs. Reaction

Unfortunately my misguided efforts to man the helm were all too typical. Clients come to see me because they feel emotionally unwell, in part because they mistakenly believe that either *they* have control over their life circumstances, or their life *circumstances* have control over them. I teach that control is when we demonstrate a healthy *response,* rather than an unhealthy *reaction* to life's circumstances. Response means *thought* before behavior. Reaction means *behavior* before thought. This can make the difference between engaging in self-focused victim behavior and God-focused victor behavior.

Once we learn what we can and can't control, we'll develop behaviors leading to healthy *self-control.* We feel empowered, perhaps for the first time. However, caution is advised at such times. If we don't communicate our new awareness to those around us, new behaviors can be perceived as threatening. It's like changing the rules of a game without telling the other players. You may feel like a winner, but unless others are aware of the new rules, everyone could end up losing.

It's like the story of a blind couple, which I sometimes share with clients. They have lived together for years in a home where the furniture sits in inappropriate places. Since they are accustomed to and comfortable with the way things are, the arrangement is harmless enough. But one day the wife regains her sight. She immediately recognizes the need to change things around and does so. When her husband walks in, he accidentally trips over the newly rearranged furniture, which surprises and frightens him. He becomes angry, since he was not informed about these changes. Under similar circumstances, any one of us would feel out of control so, rather than appreciating the reasons for the changes, we would feel threatened. Yet, who knows? Given communication about new possibilities for our "furniture arrangement," and the option to change together, we might even decide to try a fresh, different configuration ourselves.

When we expect others to make the choices *we* do and they don't, we may attempt to control the relationship through guilt or shame. This is destructive and futile. So, in addition to letting those around us know we are making changes, we also want to remember they have the right to make their own choices—and to make them in their own time.

If we really want to be healthier and to please God, no one and nothing can stop us.
If we don't want to be healthier and don't really want to please God, no one and nothing can make us.

Another way we can look at this growth process is to recognize we are actually shifting from people-pleasing to God-pleasing behaviors. Inherent in this process is still the potential displeasure and fear of those around us. If we really want to be healthier and to please God, no one and nothing can stop us. By the same token, if we don't want to be healthier and don't *really* want to please God, no one and nothing can make us. God will not overrule the free will He has given us.

Holding this attitude can make a huge difference while in the midst of an acute personal crisis. A couple I worked with recently was at great odds. They both steadfastly hung on to their points of view. The wife finally said to her husband, "We may discover in this therapy that, not only do we not *know* each other, but we may not even want to stay married to each other." This was a catalyst to being open to their differences and deciding what they ultimately wanted to do. They began to endorse each other in both their differences and similarities, resulting in the willingness to fight for and transform their marriage.

No Land in Sight

What happens when an acute or sudden crisis turns into a chronic or long-term situation? *Who is at the helm then?* What happens to our self-control? Do we run and hide below deck, or do we remain in the wheelhouse and follow God's direction, staying the course?

Most of us will survive an acute crisis. Your mind and body are designed to do so. A fear reaction will create an adrenaline rush, the body's *fight or flight* warning system. Many of us will call out an SOS to God for help at this time. When the immediate crisis is over, however, you can be left with numerous negative reactions in your soul and body. When these negative circumstances are unrelenting, adrenal fatigue from ongoing stress alerts sets in, causing both psychological and physical harm. Unwanted experiences can severely test your faith and obedience. They can also undermine the very foundation of your faith by wearing away your resolve to cooperate with God's leading, direction, and purpose for your life.

When I took the *F/V Silkie* aground, the dire situation prompted me to become *frightened* and Mark to become *angry*. Both of these responses were acute stress reactions, which were appropriate at the time because they propelled us to quickly evaluate the damages and keep the boat from sinking. However, had I not later decided to take responsibility and learn proper navigation, the chronic stress and anxiety over such an event happening again could have taken an even more serious toll on us both.

An accumulation of multiple stressors over a short period

can produce a slow or sudden onset of physical symptoms. These we sometimes ignore when not related to current psychological stresses. We may assume these symptoms are unrelated and see them as just one more stressor on the list. But, we ignore them to our peril.

Recently Ken and I experienced wave upon wave of challenges over just a few months. A son and daughter were facing divorces. There were two unexpected deaths in the extended family, plus serious diagnoses in three close friends, one that was near-death in severity. My concerns meeting a publication deadline were intense and effects from the changing economy—all things over which I had little control—felt overwhelming. In the one area of stress I *could* influence and bring some relief, I failed to do anything positive. For months, I had done nothing to help resolve my hurt feelings with a friend. Instead, I had been waiting for *her* apology. Had I done the right thing and simply spoken to and forgiven her in a timely manner, I may have prevented the health episode that followed.

One day after eating, my skin began burning, hiving, and itching all over. A routine blood test for my annual exam revealed an increase in eosinophils. Fearful of an eosinophilic gastroenteritis (EG) relapse, I reported to Ken that the food allergies and symptoms of EG were likely returning. Ken listened attentively to my growing concerns through my tears. After a time, he smiled kindly and replied, "Shelley, I think you may want to read your *own* book!" Chagrined, I really didn't want to hear what he'd just said, but I knew he was right. I was reminded that God's message in this book is about the process of living a sanctified life—the process of choosing an attitude that will honor Him, regardless of our circumstances. Oswald Chambers helped set me straight on this: "God in your life is not your relative consistency to an idea of what a believer should be, but your genuine, living relationship with Jesus Christ, and your unrestrained devotion to Him whether you are well or sick." I was humbly reminded that I, too, was human...and needed to engage my own *soul factor* continuously.

We can draw a similar analogy to chronic challenges posed by physical or psychological health issues. We can either take responsibility to learn and follow through with proper health care and spiritual practice, or remain stressed-out victims of our health challenges and poor life choices. Self-discipline and vigilance are required if we are going to get back on course...and sail on until land is in sight.

Staying the Course

Understanding that life in general is a chronic condition that ultimately leads to physical death has helped me be less fearful when I experience physical or psychological challenges. No matter what we think, do, or believe, we are all moving along the same time/space continuum. Our journey on earth *will* end in physical death. And how we choose to live affects our destiny—now, and in the spiritual dimension we're moving toward.

Life is a day-by-day adventure. It never looks like a smooth diagonal line that moves straight from the bottom left corner of a graph to the upper right-hand corner, where our physical life ends. Rather, it appears more like a jagged-toothed saw, with the outline of the blades marking the crests and troughs of the waves we encounter along the way until we enter the Father's eternal harbor.

Chronic illness can wear us out, not only physically, but also psychologically and spiritually. It is easy to understand how irrational fears and unrelieved suffering can take over the ship, and how we can revert to navigating on our own instead of following God's chosen compass setting. To get to the place where God wants us, however, we must ask Him to remain at the helm. He is Sovereign over all circumstances, and the false belief that we should be at the helm will only frustrate and set us back in our quest for Sanctification and wellness.

For many years I couldn't get past the belief that I was too broken to do anything except *perform* and *achieve* in order to gain acceptance. My purpose in life was to seek the approval of others, not God's approval. I didn't yet understand that peace would come only in knowing God would judge me, not people. So, the more I accomplished, the less I felt the love and acceptance I so desperately desired. I was the classic, unhealthy, workaholic over-achiever.

Once I began to change, moving toward God-pleasing behaviors, I started to see how *over-achieving* was harming me. Given my nature and His gifts to me, I knew God intended for me to achieve, and He created me to be creative in the process, but I was meant to do so for the purpose of His Glory, not mine.

> For to whom much is given, from Him much will be required, and to whom much has been committed, of him they will ask more. (Luke 12:48)

I needed to get clear about who I was. Only then could I understand the difference between *achieving* something for myself and *becoming* a person pleasing to God. *So, what was I supposed to do in order to really please Him?* I got a small clue from something Larry Osborne said in his great book, *The Contrarians*. "The most important thing in pleasing God is not a particular approach to spirituality or style of ministry," he said. "What matters is the fruit."

> The fruit of the Spirit is love, joy, peace, long-suffering, kindness, goodness, faithfulness, gentleness, self-control." (Galatians 22)

In time I learned I didn't have to do *everything* people expected of me in order to gain self-esteem or avoid rejection. Overdoing it only brought on fatigue and relapses of illness. Instead, I began to wait on God's leading to achieve His good purposes in my life. I saw that my *attitude,* more than my *achievements,* determines how I choose to use my thoughts, emotions, and will to overcome challenges and tap into the mind/body/Spirit connection. Whether the challenges come from me, from the world, or from God, they are my opportunity to *stay the course* and become a woman of God, which is the highest goal I can hope to achieve. Ultimately, peace comes in knowing that only God will judge me and my performance in the end, and no other.

EPILOGUE

The Ultimate Quest
Glorifying God Is the Soul's True Purpose

"But we ought always to thank God for You because from the beginning God chose you to be saved through the sanctifying work of the Spirit and through belief in the truth."

—2 THESSALONIANS 2:13

"Come, follow me," Jesus said, "and I will make you fishers of men."

—MATTHEW 4:19

When I made my maiden sea voyage aboard the *F/V Silkie*, I wasn't out on a pleasure cruise; I was learning to fish. "F/V" stands for fishing vessel. When I made my maiden voyage in writing my first book, *The Sampler*, I was also not on a pleasure cruise. I was learning about myself as I wrote down the words that expressed what I was feeling in my heart and the concepts I'd learned (and now was using) to help my clients.

I'm still learning. I am learning from God. And I am learning from clients who come seeking to learn the truth. It is not unusual for their questions and responses during therapy to reveal truths that *I* have yet to learn. We are not "captain and deck hand," but *shipmates* on a quest together.

Embarking on a spiritual quest means we've launched a fishing expedition. Christ made this very clear when he called His first disciples—four fishermen—saying, "Come, follow me, and I will make you fishers of men." As the subsequent three-and-a-half years showed, it took Peter, Andrew, James, and John a while to learn how to cast God's net properly…and for their reborn souls to go through the Sanctification process, just as we do.

We won't realize our fullest potential to glorify God without first being *in Christ* (Salvation) and then becoming *like Him* (Sanctification). Salvation is a gift, but Sanctification is a decision, a process that requires constant soul work under the guidance of the Holy Spirit. Our thoughts and emotions are influenced by our choices, and our soul makes choices that align either with the Spirit of God, the human spirit, or the spirit of the world. This *soul factor* challenges you to desire God's will for your life intensely, to choose to submit to it fully, and to listen for direction toward it continuously. As you do these things, you gradually overcome and move past obstacles (Charybdis and Scylla) and sail toward your true *home port*:

the fulfillment of God's calling for you on earth, and eternity with Him in heaven.

As believers it is our responsibility to cooperate with God as He makes us more like His Son. Remember: the purpose of Sanctification is to prepare us to be *used* by God to fulfill the mission we were created for—not to make us into perfect specimens of some useless kind.

I sometimes forget God wants us to love Him and to enjoy all of His creation while we move forward in our process. It will never be about *what* we do in our lives, but, more importantly, about *how* we do what we do in our efforts to become more like Him. This is not easy, but it *is* deeply rewarding. Though there will be work and suffering along the way and things may not always work out the way we *want,* He will map out what we need in order to accomplish His will, and He will provide it.

> *The* soul factor *challenges you to desire God's will for your life intensely, to choose to submit to it fully, and to listen for direction toward it continuously.*

I want to remember what He has already done for me—and for you. God chose to come to earth and become a human being so that He could experience what it is to be *like us.* Then He sacrificed His life so we could have eternal life and be with Him forever. In accepting Him into your life—that is, by asking for forgiveness and asking Him to be your Lord and Savior—you are promised you will live eternally with Him. What happens in your life before your body dies is the process of Sanctification—a process of becoming more like Him by doing things His way, not your own.

Taking the *F/V Silkie* aground was humiliating and frightening, but it inspired me to more diligently learn how to properly navigate her safely on future voyages. The process of Sanctification is similar. Our old way of thinking is revealed to be badly informed and unwise. It is humbling when we lay ourselves at God's feet, repent, and ask for forgiveness, but this is the first step toward "course correction" and attaining greater wisdom. "The fear of the Lord is the beginning of wisdom," Psalm 111:10 teaches.

For myself, I must do this every day. Genuine humility and obedience, which can never be practiced in excess, position me to receive God's forgiveness and blessing. His response to obedience, when I make that good choice, is like a quickening breeze to my becalmed and stagnant soul. Now His Spirit can set my sails in proper position to work the very Nature of Jesus in me. With new understanding and willingness to cooperate with Him by way of the mind/body/Spirit connection, I move full-speed ahead toward my final quest: the safe harbor of His perfect destiny for my life!

Devotion and prayer are the disciplines by which I seek to set my course each day. God's Word is a reminder He is not only interested in my spiritual life, but in my *entire* life. We sometimes ask the question, "What would Jesus do?" as we seek right relationships with God and others. To help me stay the course I also ask, concerning anything I am about to say or do: *will this bring glory to God?* This helps me to remember it is not the *process of Sanctification* to which I am devoted, but to *God Himself*. Otherwise, going to church and seeking to practice godly principles would be more like a religious, legalistic ritual to me than a spiritual response to an invitation to live life daily with the Captain of my Soul.

My ultimate quest is to have joy in the journey and to sail into God's harbor in the company of many souls who have come to know Him and become more like Christ themselves. My prayer today is that, through the application of principles in *The Soul Factor,* you also will be among this joyful multitude of shipmates sailing home.

A DAILY PRAYER FOR THE SOUL

Lord, I present myself to You: spirit, soul, and body.
All that I am or ever hope to be, I offer to You.
I give You this day. I give You this week. I give You my whole life.
I consecrate my life to You again today, Lord.
I commit all of my time, my talents, and my treasure to You.
I am Your own.

If there is any area of my life I am withholding from You,
Show me, and I will surrender it.
I empty myself now so You can fill me.
Fill me with Your Spirit, Lord.
Fill me with Your motives, Your thoughts, Your Words, and Your Deeds.
I die again to self and sin so that You can live in me.

—AUTHOR UNKNOWN

About the Author

Shelley Maurice-Maier first received Christ as her personal Savior in her 30s, but it wasn't until she had a miraculous healing herself, years later, that she began to fully understand how God was working in her life. On her journey to becoming a Christian-based psychotherapist, Maurice-Maier experienced early childhood molestation, chronic illness, cancer, seven major surgeries, divorce and a near-death experience.

Since 1983, Shelley Maurice-Maier has been a board certified, licensed Physician's Assistant (PA) in family medicine, with special interests in women's health, chronic illness, pain control, grief counseling, anxiety and depression. In 1994, the focus of her practice changed after she received a healing from the autoimmune disorder, eosinophilic gastroenteritis (EG), she had had since childhood.

She received further training in Eriksonian mental health counseling, and was granted an extended medical practice description of "insight behavioral psychotherapist" by the Oregon Board of Medical Examiners. She is the only PA psychotherapist in the country with that distinction.

"Although not completely cured from other ongoing medical challenges, I no longer have debilitating symptoms and pain from the EG. I believe the medicines I take each day are a part of God's natural healing process as well as providing for my continuing recovery and wellness, as are my thoughts and feelings about my health. The most important part of this process is that I feel *spiritually* healed. When I finally grasped the difference God's Forgiveness and Salvation could make in my physical and mental health, I choose to submit the remainder of my personal and professional life to His service."

After her healing, Maurice-Maier dedicated her life to sharing her spiritual insights with others through her counseling practice. "Rather than simply listening and attending to my patients' anatomical hearts, my passion was to focus on their psychological and spiritual hearts as well," she said. As she evolved into a Christ-focused therapist, Maurice-Maier discovered the power of understanding the "soul work" necessary to complement psychological, physical and spiritual healing.

"My therapeutic techniques now incorporate Scripture, and during a session I make every effort to treat my clients as active, not passive recipients of God's Word," she said.

About the Author

Maurice-Maier's new book, *The Soul Factor,* educates the reader about the importance of the Holy Spirit's role in our soul's work toward health and healing. She defines the "soul" as an individual's thoughts (intellect), will and emotions.

"Ultimately, it's our responsibility to chose to influence our soul by submitting it to God's word so we can become healthier human beings, capable of doing His will. I call this "the soul factor," she said. Her first book, *The Sampler: Ten Life-Enhancing Concepts Right at Your Fingertips,* uses biblical insights and life stories as a guide to living a healthier, happier life by making better mental, physical and spiritual choices. The Soul Factor delves even more deeply into the difference a personal relationship with Christ can make on our entire well being.

Shelley is a gracious, warm and compassionate therapist with a great sense of humor. She lives with her husband, Kenneth Maier, M.D. in Bend, Oregon where she is an inspirational speaker, an accomplished singer, avid horsewoman and community volunteer. Her practice, The Heart of Health, Inc. conducts workshops and retreats through her ministry, The Heart of Hope and Healing, communicating God's message of love and forgiveness to those interested in getting to the *heart* of hope and healing.

For more information:

www.theHeartofHopeandHealingministry.com
or
www.shelleymauricemaier.com